Learning Mongoid

Build scalable, efficient Rails web applications
with Mongoid

Gautam Rege

BIRMINGHAM - MUMBAI

Learning Mongoid

First published: December 2013

Production Reference: 1051213

Published by Packt Publishing Ltd.
Livery Place
35 Livery Street
Birmingham B3 2PB, UK.

ISBN 978-1-78216-750-1

www.packtpub.com

Cover Image by Aniket Sawant (aniket_sawant_photography@hotmail.com)

Credits

Author
Gautam Rege

Reviewers
Ravil Bayramgalin

Simone Carletti

Sergio Tulentsev

Acquisition Editors
Pramila Balan

Subho Gupta

Commissioning Editor
Govindan K

Technical Editors
Dipika Gaonkar

Kapil Hemnani

Nikhil Potdukhe

Copy Editors
Roshni Banerjee

Mradula Hegde

Dipti Kapadia

Kirti Pai

Lavina Pereira

Laxmi Subramanian

Project Coordinator
Joel Goveya

Proofreader
Chris Smith

Indexer
Monica Ajmera Mehta

Production Coordinator
Arvindkumar Gupta

Cover Work
Arvindkumar Gupta

About the Author

Gautam Rege is driven by his passion for programming, he co-founded Josh Software with Sethupathi Asokan in 2007. He still codes religiously and leads the marketing of the India-based Josh Software brand across the world, apart from being involved in delivering web solutions for the client partners of the organization. With more than 13 years of experience in the industry, he has handled a wide array of profiles that have helped him to develop strong analysis and project management skills, and an understanding of client partner needs for sustainable and high-standard web solutions.

He is an ardent promoter of Ruby on Rails and leads many of the brand's initiatives to promote this framework in India. He helps organize the annual RubyConf India, talks at Ruby conferences across the world, and manages local Ruby meetings. When not discussing Ruby, he loves talking about entrepreneurship and the importance of starting up young! Apart from being an active voice through his popular blog, he has authored the book *Ruby and MongoDB Web Development Beginner's Guide*, *Packt Publishing*. He truly believes that Ruby is the language of the next generation of web application development.

Before beginning his professional career in 2000, he completed his B.E. from the Pune Institute of Computer Technology (PICT). In his spare time, apart from spending time with his family, he is an athlete and loves playing cricket, basketball, and soccer when he can. He is always on the lookout to feed his hunger for adventure by going for activities such as skydiving and bungee jumping.

Writing your second book is always easier than the first because one is already tuned to write late in the night and on weekends. This book has a lot of input from practical experiences I had while working at Josh. Without the support of Sethu to free up my work so that I could find time to write this book, it may never have been completed!

My wife Vaibhavi and daughter Swara provided a lot of moral support and both were very patient even when I missed out on family time and family occasions. Thank you very much! The book reviewers and technical editors provided excellent feedback and suggestions that have helped in my work.

About the Reviewers

Simone Carletti has been working professionally with Ruby since 2006. He's very passionate about code quality and best practices.

He has been involved with free and open source software (FOSS) for more than a decade, contributing code and creating libraries in several different programming languages. The most recent projects are available in his GitHub account (weppos).

Currently, he is working as a Software Developer at DNSimple—a company providing DNS hosting, domain registration, and SSL certificates. His personal website is `http://www.simonecarletti.com/`.

Sergio Tulentsev is an early MongoDB adopter and Mongoid fan. He has used them to build systems that handle substantial load (greater than 100 million hits per day). He often speaks about MongoDB at conferences and even patched it once or twice.

When not fending off bears in snowy Russia, he travels, tries new kinds of food, and learns new languages.

www.PacktPub.com

Support files, eBooks, discount offers and more

You might want to visit www.PacktPub.com for support files and downloads related to your book.

Did you know that Packt offers eBook versions of every book published, with PDF and ePub files available? You can upgrade to the eBook version at www.PacktPub.com and as a print book customer, you are entitled to a discount on the eBook copy. Get in touch with us at service@packtpub.com for more details.

At www.PacktPub.com, you can also read a collection of free technical articles, sign up for a range of free newsletters and receive exclusive discounts and offers on Packt books and eBooks.

http://PacktLib.PacktPub.com

Do you need instant solutions to your IT questions? PacktLib is Packt's online digital book library. Here, you can access, read and search across Packt's entire library of books.

Why Subscribe?

- Fully searchable across every book published by Packt
- Copy and paste, print and bookmark content
- On demand and accessible via web browser

Free Access for Packt account holders

If you have an account with Packt at www.PacktPub.com, you can use this to access PacktLib today and view nine entirely free books. Simply use your login credentials for immediate access.

Table of Contents

Preface

Learning Mongoid gives beginners a good start to building a Rails application using MongoDB with Mongoid. For intermediate and expert Ruby developers, this book provides an excellent reference for using Mongoid. The book has plenty of examples with code samples and explanations that help in understanding the various features of Mongoid.

What this book covers

Chapter 1, *What's so Awesome about Mongoid?*, explains why Mongoid is one of the popular choices for Rails applications that use MongoDB. We are also introduced to Origin and Moped, which are integral parts of Mongoid.

Chapter 2, *Mongoid Document Model*, discusses the various data types that are supported by Mongoid and how they are stored. We learn about arrays, hashes, and embedded documents. We also briefly touch upon localized storage of string.

Chapter 3, *Persisting Documents*, discusses how documents are saved, format, optimization, and even managing custom data types and their serialization. We will also learn about atomic updates, callbacks, and validations.

Chapter 4, *Mongoid Relations*, explains the various relations that are supported by Mongoid, including One-to-One, One-to-Many, recursively embedded documents, and even polymorphic relations.

Chapter 5, Querying Attributes, explains everything about searching. We take a deep dive into how Origin works and how Mongoid criteria are managed. We learn about criteria chaining, lazy evaluation, and even eager loading of related documents.

Chapter 6, Performance Tuning, deals with how we can improve performance. We learn about the various indexes and when to use the right index. We see how the identity map can help in eager loading. Finally, we learn about MapReduce and the aggregation framework, which can drastically improve performance.

Chapter 7, Mongoid Modules, introduces various modules and gems available, which can help enhance the features with Mongoid. We learn about paranoid deletes, versioning, cloning, slugs, authentication, authorization using Devise, and even uploading documents using CarrierWave.

What you need for this book

This book assumes that you are using MacOS or Ubuntu Linux. It requires the latest MongoDB 2.4.x stable version, the latest Ruby 2.0 version, the latest Rails 4 version, and the latest Mongoid 4 version.

Who this book is for

This book is intended for beginners and experts alike. For a beginner, this book serves as an excellent guide for building Rails applications with Mongoid. For an intermediate or expert user, this book serves as an excellent reference for using the various features of Mongoid.

Conventions

In this book, you will find a number of styles of text that distinguish between different kinds of information. Here are some examples of these styles, and an explanation of their meaning.

Code words in text are shown as follows: "We can include other contexts through the use of the `include` directive."

A block of code is set as follows:

```
class Address
  include Mongoid::Document

  field :street, type: String
  field :city, type: String
  field :state, type: String
  field :zipcode, type: String
  field :country, type: String

  embedded_in :author
end
```

When we wish to draw your attention to a particular part of a code block, the relevant lines or items are set in bold:

```
require File.expand_path('../boot', __FILE__)

require "action_controller/railtie"
require "action_mailer/railtie"
require "sprockets/railtie"
```

Any command-line input or output is written as follows:

```
$ ruby -v
```

New terms and **important words** are shown in bold. Words that you see on the screen, in menus or dialog boxes for example, appear in the text like this: "clicking the **Next** button moves you to the next screen".

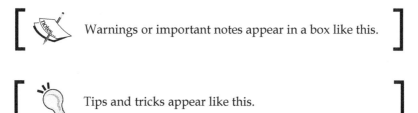

> Warnings or important notes appear in a box like this.

> Tips and tricks appear like this.

Reader feedback

Feedback from our readers is always welcome. Let us know what you think about this book—what you liked or may have disliked. Reader feedback is important for us to develop titles that you really get the most out of.

To send us general feedback, simply send an e-mail to feedback@packtpub.com, and mention the book title via the subject of your message.

If there is a topic that you have expertise in and you are interested in either writing or contributing to a book, see our author guide on www.packtpub.com/authors.

Customer support

Now that you are the proud owner of a Packt book, we have a number of things to help you to get the most from your purchase.

Downloading the example code

You can download the example code files for all Packt books you have purchased from your account at http://www.packtpub.com. If you purchased this book elsewhere, you can visit http://www.packtpub.com/support and register to have the files e-mailed directly to you.

Errata

Although we have taken every care to ensure the accuracy of our content, mistakes do happen. If you find a mistake in one of our books—maybe a mistake in the text or the code—we would be grateful if you would report this to us. By doing so, you can save other readers from frustration and help us improve subsequent versions of this book. If you find any errata, please report them by visiting http://www.packtpub.com/submit-errata, selecting your book, clicking on the **errata submission form** link, and entering the details of your errata. Once your errata are verified, your submission will be accepted and the errata will be uploaded on our website, or added to any list of existing errata, under the Errata section of that title. Any existing errata can be viewed by selecting your title from http://www.packtpub.com/support.

Piracy

Piracy of copyright material on the Internet is an ongoing problem across all media. At Packt, we take the protection of our copyright and licenses very seriously. If you come across any illegal copies of our works, in any form, on the Internet, please provide us with the location address or website name immediately so that we can pursue a remedy.

Please contact us at copyright@packtpub.com with a link to the suspected pirated material.

We appreciate your help in protecting our authors, and our ability to bring you valuable content.

Questions

You can contact us at questions@packtpub.com if you are having a problem with any aspect of the book, and we will do our best to address it.

1
What's so Awesome about Mongoid?

The name MongoDB is derived from humongous. We use DataMappers to work with MongoDB. In Ruby, the most popular MongoDB mapper is Mongoid, pronounced mann-gyod. But is this the only mapper available? There also exists MongoMapper, MongoODM, and in the realm of open source there could well be many more!

So, what is so awesome about Mongoid? In a nutshell, its ability to gel with the Rails framework makes it very popular. For me, it is this adaptability to refactor and improve that makes Mongoid a very close ally of Rails.

In this chapter, we shall get a taste of the power of Mongoid. We shall see:

- How Mongoid adheres to Rails ActiveModel and ActiveRelation syntax
- Differences between Mongoid Version 2.x and 3.x
- A brief introduction to Moped and Origin
- Some differences between MongoMapper and Mongoid and their usage

A practical approach using the Sodibee library system

Sodibee (pronounced saw-di-bee) is a library-management system that can manage books, reviews, authors, and bookings. Here are some of the functions that are supported in Sodibee:

- An author has many books and a book belongs to an author
- A book has many reviews and has one booking

- A review belongs to a user and is about a book
- A booking belongs to a user and a book

> In the course of this book we will be working with the latest versions of Ruby 2.0, Mongoid 4, Rails 4, and MongoDB 2.4.

Checking prerequisites

First and foremost, we need to ensure that we have our development environment set up. It's common to use multiple versions of Ruby for development; I use RVM to manage these versions. As we can have multiple versions of the same gem installed on our machines, we use RVM gemsets to manage the gems we need for our work.

Ruby version

To check the Ruby version, check the version that is installed using the following command:

```
$ rvm list

rvm rubies

   jruby-1.7.4 [ x86_64 ]
   ruby-1.9.3-p385 [ x86_64 ]
=* ruby-2.0.0-p247 [ x86_64 ]

# => - current
# =* - current && default
#  * - default

$ ruby -v
ruby 2.0.0p247 (2013-06-27 revision 41674) [x86_64-darwin12.4.0]
```

> Ruby 2.1 is due to be released in December, 2013. Everything in this book will be fully compatible with Ruby 2.1 too.

MongoDB version

We are currently using MongoDB v2.4.6 — verify that, using the following command:

```
$ mongo
MongoDB shell version: 2.4.6
connecting to: test
>
```

If you don't see this, it's quite likely that you have not installed MongoDB or it isn't running. Get going!

Setting up Sodibee

First and foremost, let's install the Rails gem.

```
$ gem install rails
```

This installs Rails 4.0.0.

 At the time of writing this book, the Rails version was 4.0.0. All commands would be fully compatible with the latest Rails version.

Now, let's create the Sodibee project.

```
$ rails new sodibee -O -T
```

This creates a new Rails project. The -O option tells Rails to skip ActiveRecord (we don't need it), and –T tells Rails to skip test unit. (We plan to use rspec later).

 When you run the preceding command, it initiates a bundle install and updates our bundle with the default gems. If you are as impatient as I am, you may interrupt the process and press *Ctrl + C* to stop it, as we need to modify Gemfile to add other gems anyway.

Now, open Gemfile and configure for Mongoid.

```
gem 'mongoid', git: "git://github.com/mongoid/mongoid.git"
```

 Mongoid master is currently in sync with Rails 4. So, if we install using the released gem, it will install Version 3.x.

We're almost done. Issue the following command to update the bundle with our Mongoid gem:

```
$ bundle
```

If you did not use the -O option, you can run the following instructions to remove ActiveRecord from the application as we don't need it. Check and remove database.yml under config, if it has been generated. Next ensure that application.rb under config has the following lines:

```
require File.expand_path('../boot', __FILE__)

require "action_controller/railtie"
require "action_mailer/railtie"
require "sprockets/railtie"

# Assets should be precompiled for production (so we don't need
  the gems loaded then)
Bundler.require(*Rails.groups(assets: %w(development test)))
```

Downloading the example code

You can download the example code files for all Packt books you have purchased from your account at http://www.packtpub.com. If you purchased this book elsewhere, you can visit http://www.packtpub.com/support and register to have the files e-mailed directly to you.

Notice that there is no require "rails/all". This ensures that the ActiveRecord railtie is not loaded. However, sometimes this causes a conflict with the environment settings. So, in case you face a problem starting the Rails console, remove the following line from development.rb under config/environments (and as required from the other environment files):

```
# config.active_record.migration_error = :page_load
```

This should get us going. Now issue the following command to set up Mongoid:

```
$ bundle exec rails generate mongoid:config
```

This generates mongoid.yml under config.

Test this basic Rails setup by starting the console.

```
$ rails c
Loading development environment (Rails 4.0.0)
2.0.0-p247 :001 >
```

If you see the preceding command prompt, we are set.

Creating models

Now that we have our environment set up, let's create our basic models. In the `Author` model, we shall now add a field called `name`, and create a relation between the `Author` model and the `Address` model.

```
$ rails generate model Author
# app/models/author.rb
class Author
  include Mongoid::Document
  include Mongoid::Attributes::Dynamic

  field :name, type: String

  embeds_one :address
end
```

Now, let's create the `Address` model with a number of fields and relations.

```
$ rails generate model Address
class Address
  include Mongoid::Document

  field :street, type: String
  field :city, type: String
  field :state, type: String
  field :zipcode, type: String
  field :country, type: String

  embedded_in :author
end
```

Now, let's test the code that we have written.

 Did you notice that we are not using the hash rocket (=>) notation for defining the hash of options for the `field` method? Instead of `:type => String`, we are using the JSON notation instead. We shall follow this standard throughout the book.

Testing the models

Now that we have created the models, let's test it out quickly:

```
irb> a = Author.create(name: "Charles Dickens")
 => #<Author _id: 5143678345db7ca255000001, name: "Charles Dickens">
```

```
irb> a.create_address(street: "Picadilly Circus", city: "London",
  country: "UK")
 => #<Address _id: 514367f445db7ca255000003, street: "Picadilly
  Circus", city: "London", state: nil, zipcode: nil, country: "UK">
```

As we can see, this creates an `Author` object and its corresponding `Address` object. Mongoid includes ActiveModel and you may notice the similarity in these methods if you have used ActiveRecord.

> We have used `create_address` because an author has only one embedded address. If, an author had multiple addresses, we would have used `a.addresses.create`.

```
irb> Author.first
 => #<Author _id: 5143678345db7ca255000001, name: "Charles Dickens">
```

```
irb> Author.first.address
 => #<Address _id: 514367f445db7ca255000003, street: "Picadilly
  Circus", city: "London", state: nil, zipcode: nil, country: "UK">
```

Here, we have double-checked that the author is indeed persisted to the database. Since this is MongoDB, we can dynamically add attributes to the object!

```
irb> a['language'] = "English"
 => "English"
```

```
irb> a.save
 => true
```

```
irb> Author.first
 => #<Author _id: 5143678345db7ca255000001, name: "Charles Dickens",
  language: "English">
```

Introducing Moped

So, let's see what happened in Mongoid and MongoDB. First, let's see what is in the log file `development.log` under `log`.

When we issued the command `Author.create(name: "Charles Dickens")`, it generated the following output:

```
MOPED: 127.0.0.1:27017 INSERT        database=sodibee_development
  collection=authors documents=[{"_id"=>"5143678345db7ca255000001",
  "name"=>"Charles Dickens"}] flags=[] (0.2460ms)
```

Now, when we issued the second command `a.create_address(street: "Picadilly Circus", city: "London", country: "UK")`, it updated the `Author` object, and created an embedded `Address` document as seen in the following line:

```
MOPED: 127.0.0.1:27017 UPDATE        database=sodibee_development
  collection=authors selector={"_id"=>"5143678345db7ca255000001"}
  update={"$set"=>{"address"=>{"_id"=>"514367f445db7ca255000003",
  "street"=>"Picadilly Circus", "city"=>"London", "country"=>"UK"}}}
  flags=[] (0.1211ms)
```

Now that we have seen what `INSERT` and `UPDATE` look like, querying the Author collection with `Author.first` generates the following result:

```
MOPED: 127.0.0.1:27017 QUERY         database=sodibee_development
  collection=authors selector={"$query"=>{}, "$orderby"=>{:_id=>1}}
  flags=[:slave_ok] limit=-1 skip=0 batch_size=nil fields=nil
  (66.7090ms)
```

And since we want to query the address, we look it up using `Author.first.address`. This generates the following line:

```
MOPED: 127.0.0.1:27017 QUERY         database=sodibee_development
  collection=authors selector={"$query"=>{}, "$orderby"=>{:_id=>1}}
  flags=[:slave_ok] limit=-1 skip=0 batch_size=nil fields=nil
  (0.5021ms)
```

Now there's something interesting about the preceding output—the last two commands on the `Author` model fired the same query, and look at the difference in the query result! The same query is fired because the address is an embedded document. So, to fetch the address of an author, you fetch the `Author` object itself. The difference of 66 ms and 0.5 ms in the query response is because for the first lookup MongoDB loads the document from the disk and puts it into its memory-mapped file. The second time, the document is simply looked up in cache (the memory-mapped file) and hence the lookup is faster.

Dynamic attributes

When we issued the command a['language'] = "English", and saved the object using a.save; this is what we see:

```
MOPED: 127.0.0.1:27017 UPDATE          database=sodibee_development
   collection=authors selector={"_id"=>"5143678345db7ca255000001"}
   update={"$set"=>{"language"=>"English"}} flags=[] (0.1121ms)
```

This is the result of dynamic attribute update. Even though we did not specify language as a field in the Author model, we can set it as an attribute for the Author object. Did you notice that the update for dynamic attributes is no different from the standard update query in MongoDB?

However, there is a difference when accessing it in Mongoid. The Author.first. language parameter may throw an error sometimes, but Author.first[:language] will always succeed. Let's see an example:

```
irb> a = Author.create(name: "Gautam")
 => #<Author _id: 515085fd45db7c911e000003, name: "Gautam">
```

Here we have created a new Author object. However, when we try to update the object using the dot notation a.language, it gives an error. As we can see in the following command lines, method_missing does not dynamically create the accessor method if the dynamic attribute does not already exist.

```
irb> a.language = "English"
NoMethodError: undefined method `language=' for #<Author _id:
515085fd45db7c911e000003, name: "Gautam">
   from lib/mongoid/attributes.rb:317:in `method_missing'
   from (irb):12
   from lib/rails/commands/console.rb:88:in `start'
   from lib/rails/commands/console.rb:9:in `start'
   from lib/rails/commands.rb:64:in `<top (required)>'
   from bin/rails:4:in `require'
   from bin/rails:4:in `<main>'
```

Now, if we try to update the dynamic attribute without using the dot notation, it works!

```
irb> a[:language] = "English"
 => "English"
irb> a.save
 => true
```

Since we have saved it now, when we access the dynamic attribute `language` again, `method_missing` creates the accessor method because the dynamic attribute exists. So, now even the dot notation works.

```
irb> a.language
 => "English"
irb> a[:language]
 => "English"
```

Introducing Origin

Origin is a gem that provides the DSL for Mongoid queries. Though at first glance, a question may seem to arise as to why we need a DSL for Mongoid queries; If we are finally going to convert the query to a MongoDB-compliant hash, then why do we need a DSL?

Origin was extracted from Mongoid gem and put into a new gem, so that there is a standard for querying. It has no dependency on any other gem and is a standalone pure query builder. The idea was that this could be a generic DSL that can be used even without Mongoid!

So, now we have a very generic and standard querying pattern. For example, in Mongoid 2.x we had the criteria `any_in` and `any_of`, and no direct support for the and, or, and nor operations. In Mongoid 2.x, the only way we could fire a `$or` or a `$and` query was like this:

```
Author.where("$or" => {'language' => 'English', 'address.city' =>
  'London
'})
```

And now in Mongoid 3, we have a cleaner approach.

```
Author.or(:language => 'English', 'address.city' => 'London')
```

Origin also provides good selectors directly in our models. So, this is now much more readable:

```
Book.gte(published_at: Date.parse('2012/11/11'))
```

As we shall see later in the book, Origin has a lot more cool features.

Notice about Mongoid 2.x

It's important to realize that quite a bit has changed between the two major releases of Mongoid. It's an uncanny coincidence that just like Rails, major versions (2.x and 3.x) differ from each other vastly. Let's take a look at some of the differences between Mongoid 2.x and Mongoid 3.x.

- Mongoid 3.x and later versions support Ruby 1.9.3 and onwards only.
- There are entirely new options in `mongoid.yml` for database configuration.
- Mongoid has changed its serialization mechanism.
- Apart from these, there are quite a few more changes, which have made using Mongoid better and faster.

Mongoid and MongoMapper

It's also important to know about the other Ruby ODMs (Object Document Managers) besides Mongoid. Among the most popular ones out there, is MongoMapper.

- MongoMapper, though older than Mongoid, has a slower evolution cycle. Unlike Mongoid, MongoMapper differentiates between documents and embedded documents.
- MongoMapper uses a non-ActiveModel syntax such as `many` and `one`, where Mongoid uses `has_many` and `has_one`.
- Mongoid has currently become more popular because of its adherence to the Rails ActiveModel and ActiveRelation syntax.
- Mongoid has much better documentation than MongoMapper.

Summary

Mongoid has power. Just like Rails, it evolves fast. It has Moped and Origin that ensure speed, flexibility, and consistency.

In the upcoming chapters, we shall see what documents are, in the context of Mongoid. We shall learn about the different data types, dynamic attributes, and how data is managed.

The journey has just begun.

2
Mongoid Document Model

This is where we prepare to take the deep dive. In this chapter we shall see what we mean by documents and look into some of the internal access and storage. We shall learn about the various data types including some new ones that were added to Mongoid 3.

The Mongoid document

MongoDB stores documents that have fields and maybe other documents embedded in it. The documents are stored in collections. This is analogous to records stored in tables. The difference is that documents, unlike records in a SQL database, need not have the same structure or fields. In fact, as we have already seen in the previous chapter, there is no standard structure for storing documents in MongoDB.

So, do we define a default structure when we use Mongoid? Yes, not only can we define some basic default fields in a Mongoid document but we can also add fields dynamically (we saw this in the previous chapter). So we get the best of both worlds. If you have used ActiveRecord migrations earlier, remember that we don't need them anymore as we define the default fields in the model itself.

Documents are stored in the BSON format by MongoDB. BSON (Binary JSON) is a compact format that uses JSON standards for communication, and a serialized format for storage. This gives us the ability to use arrays and hashes in MongoDB documents, which is not available in the standard SQL databases.

Now, Mongoid is a Ruby ORM and so, a Rails model needs to be enhanced to make it compatible with MongoDB. To do so, all we have to do is add `include Mongoid::Document` in our Ruby class.

Basic attributes

Mongoid supports the standard data types that MongoDB supports. This is best explained with an example:

```
class Book
  include Mongoid::Document

  field :title, type: String
  field :price, type: Float
  field :page_count, type: Integer
  field :published_date, type: Date
  field :is_best_seller, type: Boolean, default: false
end
```

As we can see, we can define strings, integers, and date fields and even set default values. Let's see how we can use these Mongoid models and the way they are stored in the database. Let's hit the rails console:

```
$ rails c

Loading development environment (Rails 4.0.0)

irb> Book.create
 => #<Book _id: 515c634c45db7c9233000001, title: nil, price: nil,
  page_count: nil, published_date: nil, is_best_seller: false>
```

All seems well. As we can see that all the fields we had defined in the model are accessible. Let's see what the MongoDB document looks like:

```
$ mongo sodibee_development

MongoDB shell version: 2.4.6

connecting to: sodibee_development

> db.books.findOne()
{ "_id" : ObjectId("515c634c45db7c9233000001"), "is_best_seller" :
  false }
```

Surprise! Here we can see only one field `is_best_seller` that is set to `false`. What happened to the other fields? After a quick gasp, I am sure you have realized what happened.

Since we had defined the default value for `is_best_seller`, the field is actually stored in the database, as the other fields did not have their defaults defined, they were not even stored. However, when Mongoid fetches the document from MongoDB and creates the `Book` Ruby object, it sets up the default accessible fields with the default value as `nil`. This ensures consistency between the different `Book` objects.

Arrays and hashes

In addition to these basic attributes, we can also define arrays and hashes. For example:

```
class Book
  include Mongoid::Document

  # ...
  field :awards, type: Array
  field :reviews, type: Hash
end
```

Let's try and see how these data types are used.

```
irb > b = Book.first
 => #<Book _id: 515c634c45db7c9233000001, title: nil, price: nil,
  page_count: nil, published_date: nil, is_best_seller: false,
  awards: nil, reviews: nil>
```

As expected, we can see that `awards` and `reviews` are set to `nil`. But now a question arises, that is, how do we save data in the array? Let's try some stunts:

```
irb> b.awards << "Booker Prize"
NoMethodError: undefined method `<<' for nil:NilClass
 from (irb):4
 from railties-4.0.0/lib/rails/commands/console.rb:88:in `start'
 from railties-4.0.0/lib/rails/commands/console.rb:9:in `start'
 from railties-4.0.0/lib/rails/commands.rb:64:in `<top (required)>'
 from bin/rails:4:in `require'
 from bin/rails:4:in `<main>'
```

This seems fair as `b.awards` is `nil`. So we have to achieve this in another way:

```
irb> b.awards = ["Booker Prize"]
 => ["Booker Prize"]
irb> b.awards << "Pulitzer Prize"
 => ["Booker Prize", "Pulitzer Prize"]
irb> b.save
 => true
```

This means we create the array first, and then insert elements in the Ruby style.

 It is a recommended practice to set the default values for arrays and hashes using `default: []` and `default: {}`, respectively.

Date and time attributes

Date and time are always tricky. Couple this with time zones, and it's crazy! For example, if it's 10 p.m. according to Indian Standard Time (GMT+5:30) and we save information to the database, it should be saved in a consistent format such that it can be read at any time even if the server is accessed in a different time zone, say GMT. So MongoDB saves everything in UTC. Mongoid automatically converts to UTC when it saves the time to the database and reconverts back to the relevant time zone when it reads back to a Ruby object.

Let's update our book with `published_date` first by firing these commands on the console:

```
irb> b.published_date = Date.today - 1.month
 => Tue, 25 Jun 2013
irb> b.save
 => true
```

Now let's query this book by firing the following command:

```
irb> Book.lte(published_date: Date.today).first
```

The query that gets fired is given as follows:

```
query sodibee_development.books query: { $query: { published_date: {
  $lte: new Date(1365206400000) } }, $orderby: { _id: 1 } }
  ntoreturn:1 keyUpdates:0 locks(micros) r:336 nreturned:1 reslen:138
  0ms
```

If we see, how this object looks on the database console, we can see how MongoDB saves it in the standard ISO format.

```
> db.books.findOne()
{
  "_id" : ObjectId("515c634c45db7c9233000001"),
  "awards" : [
    "Booker Prize",
    "Pulitzer Prize"
  ],
  "is_best_seller" : false,
  "published_date" : ISODate("2013-06-25T00:00:00Z")
}
```

Serialization with Mongoize

Mongoize was a new term coined when Mongoid 3 was introduced. The serialization process was entirely rewritten to accommodate not just the basic data types but even custom fields. So, now every native Ruby data type gets enhanced with four new methods: #mongoize, .mongoize, .demongoize, and .evolve.

 The standard nomenclature of specifying class methods is with a . prefix and instance methods with a # — so #mongoize means the instance method, while .mongoize means the class method.

This change was brought in with Mongoid 3 because it was important to support custom serialization. Let's see an example:

```
module Mongoid
  module Extensions
    module Set

      def mongoize
        ::Set.mongoize(self)
      end

      module ClassMethods
        def demongoize(object)
          ::Set.new(object)
        end

        def mongoize(object)
          object.to_a
        end
      end
    end
  end
end

::Set.__send__(:include, Mongoid::Extensions::Set)
::Set.__send__(:extend, Mongoid::Extensions::Set::ClassMethods)
```

As we can see, Mongoid::Extensions is the module that gets included and extended into the standard Ruby classes. In Mongoid 2 and earlier, this was not as structured as in the later versions. There were methods called serialize and deserialize but they were not standardized. So with new changes, Mongoid now supports even irregular data types such as Symbol, Regexp, Range, and so on.

`evolve` is a method that is supposed to resolve the data type that can be used in `Mongoid::Criteria`. This is used for querying collections. As we shall see in the later chapters, `evolve` is useful in chaining multiple criteria with custom data types.

Did you notice that in the preceding code, we don't see the `evolve` method even though this code has been picked right out of the Mongoid source code? This is because `evolve` has been subtly defined in the `origin` gem. Here is the piece of code that completes the mystery:

```
module Origin
  module Extensions

    # This module contains additional object behaviour.
    module Set
      module ClassMethods

        # Evolve the set, casting all its elements.
        def evolve(object)
          return object if !object || !object.respond_to?(:map)
          object.map{ |obj| obj.class.evolve(obj) }
        end
      end
    end
  end
end
::Set.__send__(:extend, Origin::Extensions::Set::ClassMethods)
```

The Mongoize way sets the stage for custom fields. If we want to create a custom data type, all we have to do is create a class and implement the four methods we have described before. In the preceding example, we can use the custom data type `Set` as follows:

```
class Profile
  include Mongoid::Document
  field :locations, type: Set
end
```

As you can see, we have used a custom data type that MongoDB does not support.

Field aliases

Field aliases were introduced from Mongoid 3 and they are pretty useful. We can make field aliases as shown in the following code:

```
class Book
  include Mongoid::Document

  field :t, as: :title, type: String
end
```

So the field name in the database would be t but when we access it in Mongoid, it can be accessed by the more readable :title. So you may wonder what we need this for and why? One of the advantages is that each field stored in the database is going to be smaller, but in our code we can access it with its longer name. This saves a little bit of document storage space. In the preceding example, the field will be stored in the database as t but we can access it on the object as title.

The greatest advantage of this, however, is creating a compound index. The maximum length of an index name is limited to 125 characters, and the index name is a concatenation of the field names and direction.

 The index name limit is documented as 128 characters but, in reality, it can store only 125. See https://jira.mongodb.org/browse/DOCS-1820 for details.

So if we create a compound index of fields that have long names, we would not be able to create an index easily. For example, we have the following code:

```
class Contact
  include Mongoid::Document

  field :last_name, type: String
  field :first_name, type: String
  field :middle_name, type: String
  field :title, type: String
  field :employer, type: String
  field :org_name, type: String
  field :occupation, type: String
  field :prefix, type: String
  field :suffix, type: String
  field :telephone, type: String
  field :street_1, type: String
  field :street_2, type: String
  field :city, type: String
```

```
    field :state, type: String
    field :zip_code, type: String

    index({ last_name: 1, last_name: 1, first_name: 1,
            middle_name: 1, title: 1, employer: 1,
            org_name: 1, occupation: 1, prefix: 1,
            suffix: 1, telephone: 1, street_1: 1,
            street_2: 1, city: 1, state: 1, zip_code: 1})
  end
```

[The default data type for fields is `String`, so if we don't specify a data type, it's going to be stored as a string.]

Now if we run `rake db:mongoid:create_indexes`, it will try to create the indexes and we see output that will be something as seen in the following code:

```
$ bundle exec rake db:mongoid:create_indexes
INFO -- : MONGOID: Created indexes on Book:
INFO -- : MONGOID: Index: {:t=>1}, Options: {:background=>true}
INFO -- : MONGOID: Created indexes on Contact:
INFO -- : MONGOID: Index: {:last_name=>1, :first_name=>1,
  :middle_name=>1, :title=>1, :employer=>1, :org_name=>1,
  :occupation=>1, :prefix=>1, :suffix=>1, :telephone=>1,
  :street_1=>1, :street_2=>1, :city=>1, :state=>1, :zip_code=>1},
  Options: {}
```

However, this fails silently with the exception: **exception: ns name too long, max size is 128 code:10080**. What's worse is this error does not get propagated back to Mongoid. Now let's revamp the code just a wee bit using field aliasing.

```
class Contact
  include Mongoid::Document

  field :ln, as: :last_name, type: String
  field :fn, as: :first_name, type: String
  field :mn, as: :middle_name, type: String
  field :t, as: :title, type: String
  field :e, as: :employer, type: String
  field :on, as: :org_name, type: String
  field :o, as: :occupation, type: String
  field :pr, as: :prefix, type: String
  field :su, as: :suffix, type: String
  field :te, as: :telephone, type: String
  field :st1, as: :street_1, type: String
```

```
field :st2, as: :street_2, type: String
field :c, as: :city, type: String
field :s, as: :state, type: String
field :z, as: :zip_code, type: String

index({ last_name: 1, last_name: 1, first_name: 1,
        middle_name: 1, title: 1, employer: 1,
        org_name: 1, occupation: 1, prefix: 1,
        suffix: 1, telephone: 1, street_1: 1,
        street_2: 1, city: 1, state: 1, zip_code: 1})
end
```

Notice that all we have added to this model is the as option. Now when we try to create the indexes, we will see something as in the following command:

```
$ bundle exec rake db:mongoid:create_indexes
INFO -- : MONGOID: Created indexes on Book:
INFO -- : MONGOID: Index: {:t=>1}, Options: {:background=>true}
INFO -- : MONGOID: Created indexes on Contact:
INFO -- : MONGOID: Index: {:ln=>1, :fn=>1, :mn=>1, :t=>1, :e=>1,
  :on=>1, :o=>1, :pr=>1, :su=>1, :te=>1, :st1=>1, :st2=>1, :c=>1,
  :s=>1, :z=>1}, Options: {}
```

Notice that the index name now uses the actual field names but the ruby object can be accessed via the full aliased name.

 MongoDB also supports the naming of an index when creating it. So, when we create indexes with a lot of fields, we can avoid exceeding the name limit by explicitly specifying the index name instead of letting it get autogenerated.

Embedded documents

As the name suggests, documents embedded inside other documents are called embedded documents. When the parent document is fetched, it also fetches all the embedded documents. This is similar to the composition concept.

The following code shows how we can define an embedded document:

```
class Address
  include Mongoid::Document

  field :street, type: String
```

```
    field :city, type: String
    field :state, type: String
    field :zipcode, type: String
    field :country, type: String

    embedded_in :author
  end
```

And the following code denotes how we can embed it into another model:

```
class Author
  include Mongoid::Document

  field :name, type: String

  has_many :books
  embeds_one :address
end
```

Now let's have a quick look at how this information was stored in the database. As it was an embedded document, when we fetched the author object, we also got the author's address.

```
> db.authors.findOne()
{
  "_id" : ObjectId("5143678345db7ca255000001"),
  "address" : {
    "_id" : ObjectId("514367f445db7ca255000003"),
    "street" : "Picadilly Circus",
    "city" : "London",
    "country" : "UK"
  },
  "language" : "English",
  "name" : "Charles Dickens"
}
```

This looks as expected. We can see that the address is embedded inside the Author document. Let's see, using the following command, how Mongoid handles this:

```
irb> Author.first
 => #<Author _id: 5143678345db7ca255000001, name: "Charles Dickens",
 language: "Hindi">
```

Interesting! When we fetch the `Author` document from Mongoid, we do not see the address. This is because the address is configured as a relation in the Author model. To fetch the address, we have to access the relation.

```
> Author.first.address

=> #<Address _id: 514367f445db7ca255000003, street: "Picadilly
  Circus", city: "London", state: nil, zipcode: nil, country: "UK",
  publisher_id: nil>
```

It's interesting to know that this is not a query to the database. It fetches the `Author` document and then accesses the embedded document and returns the `Address` Ruby object.

 In MongoMapper, an embedded document must include the module `MongoMapper::EmbeddedDocument`. However, in Mongoid, an embedded document includes `Mongoid::Document`.

So, does this mean that if we have a Mongoid model, it can be embedded and related to other documents at the same time? Let's see what happens.

Let's add a new model called `Publisher`.

```
class Publisher
  include Mongoid::Document

  field :name, type: String

  has_many :addresses
end
```

Here addresses are not embedded but related. Now when we try to create a `Publisher` object, Mongoid raises an error with a huge explanation of the problem, summary, and its resolution.

```
irb> Publisher.create(name: "Packt Publishing")


Mongoid::Errors::MixedRelations:

Problem:

  Referencing a(n) Address document from the Publisher document via a
    relational association is not allowed since the Address is
    embedded.
```

Summary:

    In order to properly access a(n) Address from Publisher the
      reference would need to go through the root document of Address.
      In a simple case this would require Mongoid to store an extra
      foreign key for the root, in more complex cases where Address is
      multiple levels deep a key would need to be stored for each
      parent up the hierarchy.

Resolution:

    Consider not embedding Address, or do the key storage and access in
      a custom manner in the application code.

Wow! That's indeed some error and some explanation. Let's look at it more carefully. It has raised a `Mongoid::Errors::MixedRelations` error—and rightly so. We cannot embed and relate the document. Why, you ask? Well, every model maps to a collection in MongoDB. Embedded documents reside inside a parent so they never have their own collection.

Mongoid uses the `embedded_in` relation to identify the parent document. If the `embedded_in` relation is not specified in the child model, the document cannot be saved. Mongoid uses this relation to check whether the document is an embedded document and if it is, it will complain that a relational association is not allowed since it's embedded.

If we try to create an address directly, it understandably fails with the error `Mongoid::Errors::NoParent` and again gives a detailed `Problem`, `Summary`, and `Resolution`, which can be seen as follows:

`irb> Address.create`

`Mongoid::Errors::NoParent:`

Problem:

    Cannot persist embedded document Address without a parent document.

Summary:

    If the document is embedded, in order to be persisted it must
      always have a reference to its parent document. This is most
      likely caused by either calling Address.create or Address.create!
      without setting the parent document as an attribute.

Resolution:

    Ensure that you've set the parent relation if instantiating the
      embedded document direcly, or always create new embedded
      documents via the parent relation.

Localization

MongoDB inherently supports localization and in turn, so does Mongoid. MongoDB saves localized information in a hash. We can set a fallback to a default locale by setting an option in the Rails environment, that is, `development.rb` under `config/environments` as `config.i18n.fallbacks = true`. It's pretty straightforward. First let's configure a localized field.

```
class Book
  include Mongoid::Document

  #...
  field :currency, localize: true
end
```

Now we can play around with this localized field.

```
irb> b = Book.first
 => #<Book _id: 515c634c45db7c9233000001, t(title): nil, price: nil,
page_count: nil, published_date: 2013-25-06 00:00:00 UTC, is_best_
seller: false, awards: ["Booker Prize", "Pulitzer Prize"], reviews: nil,
currency: nil, author_id: nil>
irb> I18n.locale
 => :en
irb> b.currency = "GBP"
 => "GBP"
irb> b.save
 => true
irb> I18n.locale = :hi
 => :hi
irb> b.currency = 'INR'
 => "INR"
irb> b.save
 => true
```

Now if we fetch the object again, we can see that the localized field is saved as a hash.

```
irb> b = Book.first
 => #<Book _id: 515c634c45db7c9233000001, t(title): nil, price: nil,
   page_count: nil, published_date: 2013-25-06 00:00:00 UTC,
   is_best_seller: false, awards: ["Booker Prize", "Pulitzer Prize"],
   reviews: nil, currency: {"en"=>"GBP", "hi"=>"INR"}, author_id:
   nil>
```

However, when we access the currency, we get the localized string and not the hash.

```
> b.currency
 => "INR"
> I18n.locale = :en
 => :en
> b.currency
 => "GBP"
```

So, what happens if we encounter a locale that does not have a localized value? If the fallback is not configured, it will return `nil`.

```
irb> I18n.locale = :gz
 => :gz
irb> b.currency
 => nil
```

We can enable fallbacks to ensure that we get some default. Ensure that the Rails environment, that is, `development.rb` under `config/environments` has `config.i18n.fallbacks = true` and then configure the fallbacks.

```
irb> I18n.fallbacks[:en] = [:en, :hi]
 => [:en, :hi]
irb> I18n.locale = :gz
 => :gz
2.0.0p0 :005 > Book.first.currency
 => "GBP"
```

But that's not all. We can query based on a locale.

```
irb> Book.where("currency.hi" => 'INR').first
 => #<Book _id: 515c634c45db7c9233000001, t(title): nil, price: nil,
    page_count: nil, published_date: 2013-25-06 00:00:00 UTC,
    is_best_seller: false, awards: ["Booker Prize", "Pulitzer Prize"],
    reviews: nil, currency: {"en"=>"GBP", "hi"=>"INR"}, author_id:
    nil>
```

 Ensure that the localized query is a string: `"currency.hi"` and not `:currency.hi`.

Mass assignment and security

Mass assignment of attributes is a way in which we can assign multiple attributes of an object directly. Typically, the parameter hash `params` can be used directly to update the object. For example:

```
# params: { name: "Gautam", age: 35}
User.update_attributes(params)
```

But, what happens if someone updates information that should not have been part of `params`? What if someone inserted information such as `password: "something"` into the `params` hash? It will update the `User` object and create havoc.

That's exactly what happened.

> Early in 2012, Egor Homakov hacked `github.com` using this mass assignment Rails vulnerability. He was kind enough not to cause any harm and his intention was only to highlight the Rails' vulnerability of mass assignment.
>
> He posted his own SSH key into the Rails core team user as a mass assignment, and it worked! He had full access to the repository after that. He highlighted that mass assignment is dangerous.

To protect against mass assignment, Rails introduced `attr_protected` and `attr_accessible` as the means to manage mass assignment. Since Mongoid uses Rails ActiveModel, we can protect the document attributes from mass assignment.

Rails 4 has mass assignment integrated in the core. Instead of protecting fields in our models, the Rails core team felt it necessary to prevent this early on. So, they introduced `strong_parameters` that handles data at the controller itself and prevents unpermitted parameter attributes from creeping into our controller methods. If you are using Rails 3, you may choose to include the gem `strong_parameters`, to get the same functionality.

Now this causes a huge paradigm shift from the patched `attr_accessible` that was introduced early on. So, if we want to revert back to the original mass assignment security code, we can use the gem named `protected_attributes`.

We can resolve mass assignment in two ways. First, let's use the `protected_ attributes` gem and `attr_protected` or `attr_accessible` as in the following example:

```
class User
  include Mongoid::Document

  field :password, type: String
  attr_protected :password
end
```

This will prevent `password` from being assigned via mass assignment. This does not throw any error. Instead it will simply not update it. Here's how we do this:

```
irb> a = Author.first
 => #<Author _id: 5143678345db7ca255000001, name: "Charles Dickens",
    password: nil, language: "Hindi">


irb> a.update_attributes(name: "Charles Nutter", password: 'jruby')
 => true


irb> Author.first
 => #<Author _id: 5143678345db7ca255000001, name: "Charles Nutter",
    password: nil, language: "Hindi">
```

As we can see, `password` was not updated because it was protected. `attr_accessible` works in exactly the opposite way. It specifies the fields that can be used for mass assignment.

Now, let's see the Rails 4 way.

 Rails' best practices advocate the use of `strong_parameters`.

Here we do not change our model code at all; in fact, the entire game is played in the controller code. Here is an example of the creation of an author with the author's address and books being accepted as nested attributes. The model code looks as follows:

```
class Author
  include Mongoid::Document

  field :name, type: String
```

```
field :last_name, type: String
# ...

has_many :books
embeds_one :address

accepts_nested_attributes_for :books, :address
end
```

This is no different from any normal model code. Notice that there is no use of attr_accessible or attr_protected. The following is the controller code with strong_parameters support:

```
class AuthorsController < ApplicationController


  def create
    @author = Author.new(author_params)
    if @author.save
      redirect_to authors_path
    else
      render :new
    end
  end

private
  def author_params
    params.require(:author).permit(:name, :last_name,
            :address_attributes => [:street, :city, :state,
                                    :zipcode, :country],
            :books_attributes => [:title, :price])
  end
end
```

Now if we send some unpermitted parameters, the request will be trapped at the controller itself and will not be allowed to proceed further.

Summary

In this chapter, we saw what Mongoid documents are and their various characteristics. We saw how various attributes such as arrays and hashes are stored. Using Mongoize and custom serialization, we can create new data types in Mongoid and use them in our models. We also saw things such as field aliasing, localization, and even mass assignment.

In the next chapter, we shall dig deep into Origin and see the various ways to persist data. We shall see various validations that are leveraged from ActiveModel, callbacks, and even atomic updates.

3
Persisting Documents

Till now we have seen why Mongoid is so awesome and what documents are. In this chapter we will see how the documents are persisted on the disk. Some details we will learn about are as follows:

- The various options to save documents
- The compliance of ActiveModel with callbacks and validations
- Nested attributes in Mongoid
- Atomic persistence

MongoDB persistence strategy

MongoDB saves data in memory-mapped files so that data access is faster than direct disk I/O. When some document is saved, it is written quickly to the memory and persisted to the disk lazily, usually after every 60 seconds. This ensures that we have read-and-write access to databases that is almost as fast as memory.

Let's first study the format in which data is saved in MongoDB.

Binary JSON (BSON)

MongoDB uses the JSON format for storing information. As we have seen before, a typical MongoDB document has the following structure:

```
{
  "_id" : ObjectId("5143678345db7ca255000001"),
  "address" : {
    "_id" : ObjectId("514367f445db7ca255000003"),
    "city" : "London",
    "country" : "UK",
    "street" : "Picadilly Circus",
```

```
        "zip" : 123,
        "zipcode" : "123"
    },
    "language" : "Hindi",
    "last_name" : "Nutter",
    "name" : "Charles"
}
```

However, that's not how it's stored on the disk. This is because it would be very inefficient to store information in the raw JSON format. So, MongoDB follows the BSON specifications. An example of storing {"hello":"world"} in BSON is as follows:

```
"\x16\x00\x00\x00\x02hello\x00\x06\x00\x00\x00world\x00\x00"
```

Storing data in binary format has huge benefits. Data can be manipulated easily because BSON adds length prefixes for easy traversal. It's also very efficient to encode and decode. In addition to these benefits, BSON has an extended JSON-like format and supports several extra data types that do not exist in JSON such as an ObjectId!

Memory maps, delayed sync, and journals

As we have seen earlier, MongoDB stores data in memory-mapped files of at most 2 GB each. After the data is loaded for the first time into the memory mapped files, we now get almost memory-like speeds for access instead of disk I/O, which is much slower. These memory-mapped files are preallocated to ensure that there is no delay of the file generation while saving data.

However, to ensure that the data is not lost, it needs to be persisted to the disk. This is achieved by journaling. With journaling, every database operation is written to the oplog collection and that is flushed to disk every 100 ms. Journaling is turned on by default in the MongoDB configuration. This is not the actual data but the operation itself. This helps in better recovery (in case of any crash) and also ensures the consistency of writes. The data that is written to various collections are flushed to the disk every 60 seconds. This ensures that the data is persisted periodically and also ensures the speed of data access is almost as fast as memory. MongoDB relies on the operating system for the memory management of its memory-mapped files. This has the advantage of getting inherent OS benefits as the OS is improved. Also, there's the disadvantage of lack of control on how memory is managed by MongoDB.

However, what happens if something goes wrong (server crashes, database stops, or disk is corrupted)? To ensure durability, whenever data is saved in files, the action is logged to a file in a chronological order. This is the journal entry, which is also a memory-mapped file but is synced with the disk every 100 ms. Using the journal, the database can be easily recovered in case of any crash. So, in the worst case scenario, we could potentially lose 100 ms of information. This is a fair price to pay for the benefits of using MongoDB.

> MongoDB journaling makes it a very robust and durable database. However, it also helps us decide when to use MongoDB and when not to use it. 100 ms is a long time for some services, such as financial core banking or maybe stock price updates. In such applications, MongoDB is not recommended.
>
> For most cases that are not related to heavy multi-table transactions like most financial applications MongoDB can be suitable.

All these things are handled seamlessly, and we don't usually need to change anything. We can control this behavior via the configuration of MongoDB but usually it's not recommended. Let's now see how we save data using Mongoid.

Creating documents

Mongoid adheres to ActiveModel for managing objects and mapping them to MongoDB. Before we continue, it's important to realize the difference between Ruby objects and their corresponding MongoDB documents. Typically, when we use Mongoid, we deal with objects and let Mongoid manage the database persistence. Basically, we create objects and update their attributes, and this data will be saved and retrieved seamlessly.

> Creating a Ruby object does not mean it is saved to the database!

When we want to ask Mongoid to persist the Ruby object to the database, we invoke the save method. So, if we have an Author class and a corresponding object of this class, in order to persist that object, we can simply save it.

```
class Author
  include Mongoid::Document

  field :name, type: String
end
```

That one statement include Mongoid::Document is all we require to ensure that the Author class is now "MongoDB compatible". We don't have to do anything different than what we do while creating Ruby objects and invoking save.

```
$ rails c
```

```
irb> a = Author.new(name: "Gautam Rege")
=> #<Author _id: 518dfdcf45db7c6909000001, name: "Gautam Rege">
```

```
irb> a.save
=> true
```

Mongoid supports all the standard commands that are recommended by ActiveModel. So, if you are well versed with ActiveRecord or DataMapper, this is a breeze.

When Mongoid saves data, it figures out which attributes have changed and updates only them. It does not save the entire document every time, that is, it's not a **unmarshal-update-marshal** operation!

Updating documents and attributes

As with ActiveModel specifications, save will update the changed attributes and return the updated object, otherwise it will return false on failure. The save! function will raise an exception on the error. In both cases, if we pass validate: false as a parameter to save, it will bypass the validations.

A lesser-known persistence option is the upsert action. An upsert action creates a new document if it does not find it and overwrites the object if it finds it. A good reason to use upsert is in the find_and_modify action.

For example, suppose we want to reserve a book in our Sodibee system, and we want to ensure that at any one point, there can be only one reservation for a book. In a traditional scenario:

- **t1**: Request-1 searches for a for a book which is not reserved and finds it
- **t2**: Now, it saves the book with the reservation information
- **t3**: Request-2 searches for a reservation for the same book and finds that the book is reserved
- **t4**: Request-2 handles the situation with either error or waits for reservation to be freed

So far so good! However in a concurrent model, especially for web applications, it creates problems.

- **t1**: Request-1 searches for a book which is not reserved and finds it
- **t2**: Request-2 searches for a reservation for the same book and also gets back that book since it's not yet reserved
- **t3**: Request-1 saves the book with its reservation information
- **t4**: Request-2 now overwrites previous update and saves the book with its reservation information

Now we have a situation where two requests think that the reservation for the book was successful and that is against our expectations. This is a typical problem that plagues most web applications. The various ways in which we can solve this is discussed in the subsequent sections.

Database locks and transactions

Most databases lock while writing data. In SQL-based databases, there are varying levels of locking; rows, tables, or databases. Whenever there is a table level lock, it means that only one entity can access the database. So, if the database has transaction support, we can create a record and be guaranteed about the atomicity. In fact, most ACID databases that support transactions support multiple operations in a single transaction.

Applications and lock versioning

In most ACID databases, we add a new column, `lock_version INT` in the table. We ensure that we increment the column while reading it and that the same value exists when we update the column. If the version changes, it means that someone else tried accessing it. In Rails, if we simply add this column, lock versioning automatically kicks in.

The MongoDB findAndModify method

The `findAndModify` method finds the document, updates it, and returns it in a single atomic operation. This means if we simple fire the following query in the preceding scenario, we are guaranteed atomicity:

```
irb> Book.where(title: "Aristortle").find_and_modify({"$set" => {
reserved: true, reserved_by: "Willie G. Bach" } }, new: true)


 => #<Book _id: 516e7ab045db7cd86a000001, t(title): "Aristortle", price:
nil, page_count: nil, published_date: 2012-05-20 00:00:00 UTC, is_best_
seller: true, reserved: true, reserved_on: nil, reserved_by: "Willie G.
Bach", currency: nil, author_id: nil>
```

Remember that the `Book` object that is returned will return the updated document only if we set the `new: true` option. Otherwise, it will modify the document but return the original document.

Atomic attribute updates

For any atomic increments in databases, for example, maybe invoice numbers, Mongoid has atomic increment operations such as increment and decrement and even bit-wise operations.

```
irb> b = Book.last
=> #<Book _id: 516e7ab045db7cd86a000001, ... >


irb> b.inc(reserved_count: 1)
=> #<Book _id: 516e7ab045db7cd86a000001, ..., reserved_count: 1 >


irb> b.inc(reserved_count: 1)
=> #<Book _id: 516e7ab045db7cd86a000001, ..., reserved_count: 2 >


irb> b.inc(:reserved_count: -1)
=> #<Book _id: 516e7ab045db7cd86a000001, ..., reserved_count: 1 >
```

As you can see, when we call the `inc` method, it atomically updates the attribute in the databases. We do not need to call `save` on the object. Also, note the subtle syntax of decrementing using `inc` with `-1`.

We can also do bit operations atomically; for example, we have the status field on a book and we have the following bit fields:

```
RESERVED  = {or:  0b0010}
PUBLISHED = {or:  0b0001}
DAMAGED   = {or:  0b1000}


UNRESERVED = {and: 0b1101}
```

Now, we can set and reset bit fields in a status field using these various options and manage different states of the book. So, if a book is returned and is damaged, we don't want to reserve it and set the damaged bit.

```
b = Book.last
b.bit(:status, UNRESERVED)
b.bit(:status, DAMAGED)
```

Alternatively, we could also have written this by merging two of the hashed values together like this `b.bit(:status, UNRESERVED.merge(DAMAGED))`, but be careful! If we want to set the RESERVED and PUBLISHED field, this would merge {or: 0b0010} and {or: 0b0001}, and the RESERVED value would be ignored; it's a hash with the same key!

 MongoDB only supports the :and and :or bit operators, not the others.

Dynamic attributes

We have seen that MongoDB supports dynamic fields, that is, we do not have to specify any structure for documents. However, when we are using Mongoid, we can specify fields in the model. In Mongoid 4, adding dynamic attributes is prevented by default. So, if we need to support dynamic attributes, we need to include the module to support this.

```
class Book
  include Mongoid::Document
  include Mongoid::Attributes::Dynamic


  ...
  end
```

Now, we can add dynamic attributes to the Book model.

Nested attributes

It's quite common to want to create an `Author` object and the author's books at the same time. Mongoid supports the same syntax as `ActiveModel` for nested attributes. So, if you want to use nested attributes, you can simply do something as follows:

```
class Author
  include Mongoid::Document

  field :name, type: String

  has_many :books
  embeds_one :address

  accepts_nested_attributes_for :books, :address
end
```

Now, in the views, you can use the standard ActionView, `fields_for`, and use nested attributes easily.

```
<% form_for(@author) do |f| %>
  <div class='field'>
    <%= f.label :name %>
    <%= f.text_field :name %>
  </div>

  <h3> Address </h3>
  <%= f.fields_for :address do |a| %>
    <div class='field'>
      <%= a.label :street %>
      <%= a.text_field :street %>
    </div>
```

In the next chapter we shall learn about relations with Mongoid. Nested attributes in Mongoid are supported on other relations too, such as `belongs_to`, `has_and_belongs_to_many`, `embedded_in`.

There are interesting options that can be specified for nested attributes to control them.

The `:reject_if` object allows us to reject nested attributes; for example, the following example will reject the address attribute if all the fields are blank.

```
accepts_nested_attributes_for :address, reject_if: :all_blank
```

We can also specify specific constraints to reject the nested attributes; for example, reject the address if the country field is blank.

```
accepts_nested_attributes_for :address, reject_if: ->(attrs) {
attrs[:country].blank? }
```

The `:allow_destroy` object allows us to destroy a nested attribute.

The `:limit` object allows us to specify the maximum limit of nested attributes after which an error is raised.

You can read a lot more about `accepts_nested_attributes_for` at `http://api.rubyonrails.org/classes/ActiveRecord/NestedAttributes/ ClassMethods.html`.

Validations

Mongoid includes `ActiveModel::Validations`, so we have access to all the `ActiveModel` validations that are available. In a nutshell, validations ensure the sanity of the data being stored. To quote a quick example:

```
class Author
  include Mongoid::Document

  field :name, type: String

  validates :name, presence: true
end
```

This ensures that no author object will be created without a name. Similarly, there are options such as, `:uniqueness`, `:acceptance`, `:associated`, `:confirmation`, which are from `ActiveModel::Validations`, that allow checks for uniqueness of attributes, presence of associated models, and so on. The common options used along with these validations are `:if`, `:allow_nil`, and `:on`. You can find a lot more details about validations at `http://api.rubyonrails.org/classes/ActiveModel/ Validations/ClassMethods.html`.

Callbacks

Callbacks are pretty interesting in Mongoid. Just as validations, Mongoid leverages `ActiveModel::Callbacks`. Callbacks are methods that are called along with persistence. This helps us manipulate the data. We can implement various callbacks such as `before_save`, `after_create`, and `before_destroy`. The entire list of callbacks is available at `http://api.rubyonrails.org/classes/ActiveRecord/Callbacks.html`.

> Did you know `ActiveModel::Callbacks` include `after_initialize`, `after_find`, `after_touch`, `after_commit`, and `after_rollback`? Of course, `after_commit` and `after_rollback` are specific to transactional databases unlike MongoDB.

Mongoid also supports `before_upsert`, `after_upsert`, and `around_upsert`! As we have seen earlier, an upsert means "update if the document exists and create if it doesn't exist". However, there's more to callbacks in Mongoid.

Mongoid also supports the `after_add`, `after_remove`, `before_add`, and `before_remove` callback for some specific relations. Let's dive deeper into this. It happens quite often that we want to do some post-processing when a child relation is added; for example, we want to set some fields, update some counters, or maybe even check the status of the child object, and then update the parent!

```ruby
class Author
  include Mongoid::Document

  has_many :books, after_add: :send_email


  def send_email(book)
    puts "Send email: #{book.inspect}"
  end
end
```

Now, when a `Book` document gets created, the `send_email` callback gets called. This helps us do some post-processing on the child object as well as the parent object after a child is added!

Summary

In this chapter we have seen how documents are stored in MongoDB as well as how to create documents using Mongoid. We saw what atomic updates are as well as how to set nested attributes. Lastly, we took a quick look at validations and callbacks.

In the next chapter, we will study the various relations in detail and how they are managed.

4
Mongoid Relations

Now that we have seen how documents are stored, let's see how documents are related to each other. Mongoid tries to be as close to ActiveRecord relations as possible. In this chapter, we will see the basic relations that exist between documents:

- One-to-One (1-1) relation
- One-to-Many (1-N) relation
- Many-to-Many (N-N) relation
- Polymorphic relation

In addition to this, we will also learn about relations with embedded documents and how they are managed.

Configuring relationships

Before we study the methods in detail, we need to understand that all relations can specify the parameters that configure the relation. Each relation follows the following pattern:

- `name`: This is the mandatory name of the relation and is a symbol by which the relation will be referenced.
- `options`: This is a hash that is used to configure the relation.
- `block`: This is an optional block of code to configure some relations.

Common options for all relations

The following options are common to all relations:

- `:class_name`: This is the class name if it cannot be determined from the name.
- `:inverse_of`: This is the reverse relation, it is very important for creating or embedding relations.
- `:extend`: If we need to configure the relation by passing a block, a module is created on the fly with this block and the relation class then extends from this module.
- `:inverse_class_name`: This is used to determine the foreign key.
- `:name`: This is the name of the relation.
- `:relation`: This is the type of the relation. (`Referenced::One`, `Embedded::In`, among others).

 Among these options, `:name`, `:extend`, `:inverse_class_name`, and `:relation` are used internally and cannot be set. In case we define a new relationship strategy, these would be used to configure the internal MetaData class.

:class_name

If the related model cannot be deduced from the name, we would need to specify the following option:

```
class Author
  include Mongoid::Document

  has_many :self_help_books, class_name: "Book"
end
```

Here, when we access the `self_help_books` relation, the `Book` class and its collection would be accessed.

:inverse_of

In a Many-to-Many relation, Mongoid saves the information in both models. `:inverse_of` is the option that identifies the method in the other relation that is saving the data. We shall see a more detailed example of the Many-to-Many relation later.

Relation-specific options

Some of the following options are applicable to each relation. As we study the relations, we will see which options are applicable to which relations. The summary of what they mean is given in the following list:

- `:as`: This option is required while defining polymorphic relations.

- `:autosave`: This option saves the related child automatically when the parent is saved.

- `:autobuild`: This option allows a child to be build if the value in the parent is nil.

- `:primary_key`: This options allows the relation to set the primary key, which is `_id` by default.

- `:touch`: This updates the `updated_at` timestamp for the parent when the child object is touched.

- `:dependent`: This option is used to destroy all child objects just like a cascaded delete. It can have any of the following values: `:delete`, `:destroy`, `:nullify`, and `:restrict`.

- `:foreign_key`: This option indicates an explicitly defined foreign key.

- `:order`: This option sets the default order for the relation.

- `:counter_cache`: This option increments a cached counter atomically in the parent when a child is added or removed.

- `:index`: This option indicates the indexed relation field.

- `:validate`: True or false are the values for this option. This is true by default as we validate the relation for child objects.

- `:polymorphic`: This option specifies whether the relation is a polymorphic relation.

- `:cyclic`: This option specifies whether a relation is a cyclic embedded relation.

- `:cascaded_callbacks`: This option invokes cascaded callbacks on embedded objects.

- `:store_as`: This is the key for which the embedded document is saved.

- `:versioned`: This option helps manage versions of embedded documents.

In addition to these options, some relations also support callbacks that would be invoked when relations are added or removed.

- `:before_add`
- `:before_remove`
- `:after_add`
- `:after_remove`

We will see which configuration is applicable to which relation, look into their details, and study the various relations.

has_one – the one-to-one relation

As the method name suggests, `has_one` sets up the parent relation for a model having only one child:

```
class Book
  include Mongoid::Document

  has_one :book_detail
end
```

This implies that "A `Book` class has one `BookDetail`". For every parent relation, it is advisable to set the child relationship too.

```
class BookDetail
  include Mongoid::Document

  belongs_to :book
end
```

The `has_one` method takes the options discussed in the following sections.

:as

When a relation is a polymorphic relation, we need to use this option:

```
class Ship
  include Mongoid::Document

  has_one :vehicle, as: resource
end
```

This tells the `has_one` method that the vehicle is a polymorphic relation that can be accessed via the `resource_type` and `resource_id` fields in the vehicles collection. It's important that the inverse relation sets `polymorphic: true`, and we will see polymorphic relations soon.

:autosave

The `:autosave` option is `false` by default. When the object is created, the related child objects are also created. However, if the object is updated, only the object is updated and not the children.

:autobuild

If the `:autobuild` option is set to `true`, the child object will be automatically instantiated if there are no children. This is applicable only for the `has_one` or `embeds_one` relation.

:dependent

The `:dependent` option is used for cascaded deletion. That means that when the parent object is removed, we can decide how the children should be managed. We can specify various values:

- `:delete`: This deletes the relation but does not invoke the callback.
- `:destroy`: This deletes the relation and also invokes the callbacks.
- `:nullify`: This is used only for embedded documents. When this is specified, the embedded document reference is set to nil.
- `:restrict`: This will prevent a document form being deleted if it has valid children.

:primary_key

In the parent relation, the default primary key is `_id`. However, if a different key has been configured for the children, we can specify this key when accessing a relation. For example, if we want to use the ISBN (which is unique) of a book in a relation with `BookDetail`, we can specify the following relation:

```
class Book
  include Mongoid::Document

  has_one :book_detail, primary_key: :isbn
```

```
  end

class BookDetail
    include Mongoid::Document

    belongs_to :book, primary_key: :isbn
end
```

Now, when we access the `BookDetail#book_id`, it will match the ISBN and return the relevant book.

:foreign_key

In the child relation, if the reference to the parent is stored in a nonstandard key name (that is, the child relation does have the `<parent>_id` prefix), we need to specify it. For example, if a `Book` method has one `BookDetail`, but the `BookDetail` object stores the `Book#id` in `:book_detail_info`, we configure it as follows:

```
class Book
    include Mongoid::Document

    has_one :book_detail, foreign_key: :book_detail_info
end
```

Now, we cannot access the `BookDetail#book_id`, but we have to access `BookDetail#book_detail_info` instead, which saves the `Book#id` in it.

:validate

This option validates the child objects just like the `validates_associated` method. It is always turned on by default.

```
class Book
    include Mongoid::Document

    has_one :book_detail, validate: false
end
```

In a normal situation, the `book_detail` object will be validated if it is provided and an error will be returned if the validation fails. However, in the preceding case, the validation will be bypassed since it is set to false.

has_many – the many-to-one relation

The Many-to-One relation is among the most commonly used relations between documents. This is easiest seen in our previous example of authors, and how they are related to their books.

```
# app/models/author.rb

class Author
  include Mongoid::Document

    has_many :books
end

# app/models/book.rb

class Book
  include Mongoid::Document


  belongs_to :author
end
```

Though it seems very simple at first, let's look a few nuances that are commonly misunderstood.

Notice the model filename is always singular (`author.rb`, `book.rb`) as is the name of the model—`Author` and `Book`.

Remember, `has_many` is a method that creates an instance method called `books` when the `Author` class is loaded. Similarly, `belongs_to` is a method that creates an instance method called `author` when the `Book` class is loaded.

The relation names are used to infer the model name. So, using the symbols `:books` and `:author`, ActiveSupport inflector methods can find out the model names `Book` and `Author` respectively. If we have different names for the relation and the class, it needs to be configured. For example:

```
class Author
  include Mongoid::Document

  has_many :publications, class_name: 'Book'
end
```

It is also not necessary to always specify both sides of the relation, but it is recommended.

The `has_many` method takes the following options in addition to `:as`, `:autosave`, `:validate`, `:dependent`, `:primary_key`, and `:foreign_key`.

:order

We can specify the `order` object in a relation as follows:

```
class Author
  include Mongoid::Document

  has_many :books, order: { title: 1 }
end
```

This will get the books of an author sorted by `title` in ascending order!

:before_add, :after_add, :before_remove, and :after_remove

Callbacks on the relations are: `:before_add`, `:after_add`, `:before_remove`, and `:after_remove`. When we set these options, we can manage the parent and the child, before and after a relation is added or removed. Let's see a quick example of this:

```
class Author
  include Mongoid::Document

  has_many :books, after_add: :send_email

  def send_email(document)
    puts "Send email: #{document.inspect}"
    puts "self: #{self.inspect}"
  end
end
```

Now, the `send_email` callback is called with the child object whenever a book is created. Let's take a closer look.

```
irb> a = Author.last

=> #<Author _id: 519ba17d45db7c5ac9000005, name: "after1", last_name: nil, wallet: nil, password: nil>
```

```
> a.books.create

Send email: #<Book _id: 51b2ffbe45db7cb20d000001, t(title): nil,
published_date: nil, is_best_seller: false, awards: [], reviews: nil,
currency: nil, author_id: "519ba17d45db7c5ac9000005">

self: #<Author _id: 519ba17d45db7c5ac9000005, name: "after1", last_name:
nil, wallet: nil, password: nil>

 => #<Book _id: 51b2ffbe45db7cb20d000001, t(title): nil, published_date:
nil, is_best_seller: false, awards: [], reviews: nil, currency: nil,
author_id: "519ba17d45db7c5ac9000005">
```

Notice that when a book is created for an author, the `send_email` callback is called on the `Author` object. However, unlike the `ActiveModel::Callbacks` relation, the parameter passed to the object is the `Book` child object. This helps us manage pre- and post-processing when relations are added or removed.

The belongs_to relation

The `belongs_to` relation is the child side of the relation. It is set to complement the `has_one` or `has_many` relations. This method takes the following options in addition to `:autosave`, `:autobuild`, `:dependent`, `:primary_key`, and `:foreign_key`.

:index

The `index` option determines if the foreign key is indexed or not. It's recommended that foreign keys must be indexed. The values are set to true or false as shown in the following code:

```
class Book
  include Mongoid::Document

  belongs_to :author, index: true
end
```

:polymorphic

This is used to complement the `:as` option for the parent relationship. This option sets the polymorphic resource as follows:

```
class Vehicle
  include Mongoid::Document

  belongs_to :resource, polymorphic: true
end
```

:touch

The `touch` method allows the child object to update the `updated_at` field of the parent when the child is changed.

:counter_cache

When we add or remove a child, we often require the parent object to be updated with a counter. This increment or decrement is atomic. This can work with embedded objects too. Let's see an example:

```
class Author
  include Mongoid::Document
  ...

    field :books_count, type: Integer, default: 0
end

class Book
  include Mongoid::Document

  belongs_to :author, counter_cache: :books_count
end
```

Let's see how this works!

```
irb> a = Author.last
 => #<Author _id: 51b42d4245db7c9535000001, name: "Aldo", last_name:
"Manning", password: nil>


irb> a.books << Book.new(title: "How to race a mule!")
```

```
=> [#<Book _id: 51b75e6345db7c8bca000001, t(title): "How to race a
mule!", published_date: nil, is_best_seller: false, awards: [], reviews:
nil, currency: nil, author_id: "51b42d4245db7c9535000001">]
```

```
irb> a
```

```
=> #<Author _id: 51b42d4245db7c9535000001, name: "Aldo", last_name:
"Manning", password: nil, books_count: 1>
```

We can see in the preceding command that the `:books_count` field has got
incremented in `Author`. An interesting thing to consider: Do we have to create
the `:books_count` field in the `Author` model?

No. If we add dynamic attributes support to Author, the `books_count` will
automatically get created.

```
class Author
  include Mongoid::Document
  include Mongoid::Attributes::Dynamic

    . . .
  end
```

Now, when a book is created, if `:books_count` does not exist, it will get created.

has_and_belongs_to_many – the many-to-many relation

Let's assume that books belong to many categories and categories have many
books. This is the Many-to-Many relationship method. A typical class would
look like the following:

```
class Book
  include Mongoid::Document

  has_and_belongs_to_many :categories
end

class Category
  include Mongoid::Document

  has_and_belongs_to_many :books
end
```

It takes all the standard options such as `:autosave`, `:dependent`, `:foreign_key`, `:index`, `:primary_key`, and `:order`. It also supports the `:before_add`, `:after_add`, `:before_remove`, and `:after_remove` relation callbacks.

 A Many-to-Many relation cannot be a part of a polymorphic relation. This is because a polymorphic relation expects an explicit parent-child relationship and Many-to-Many relations are peer relations.

:inverse_of

Among all the other options, the `inverse_of` relation is a very interesting one. As with Many-to-Many relations, the document IDs are stored as arrays on both sides of the association. So, the `Category` and `Book` objects shown previously, `book_ids` and `category_ids` are arrays that store the `ObjectId` values of the other relations. Let's see the basic Many-to-Many relation setup. Execute the following commands:

```
irb> b = Book.first
=> #<Book _id: 4e86e45efed0eb0be0000010, _type: nil, title: nil,
publisher: "Dover Publications", name: "Oliver Twist">


irb> c = Category.first
 => #<Category _id: 4e86e4cbfed0eb0be0000012, _type: nil, name:
"Fiction">


irb> > c.books << Book.first
 => [BSON::ObjectId('4e86e45efed0eb0be0000010')]


irb> b.categories << c
 => [BSON::ObjectId('4e86e4cbfed0eb0be0000012')]


irb> b
 => #<Book _id: 4e86e45efed0eb0be0000010, _type: nil, title: nil,
publisher: "Dover Publications", category_ids: [BSON::ObjectId('4e86e4cbf
ed0eb0be0000012')], name: "Oliver Twist">


irb> c
 => #<Category _id: 4e86e4cbfed0eb0be0000012, _type: nil, name:
"Fiction", book_ids: [BSON::ObjectId('4e86e45efed0eb0be0000010')]>
```

Here we see that both the related objects — `Book` and `Category`, keep
arrays — `[BSON::ObjectId()]` that contain `ObjectId` references of each other.

The `inverse_of` option helps us configure this a little more. If we want only
one-sided references to be stored, we can set this flag to false. By default the flag
would be true. In this case, if we did not want to store the `category_ids` in the
`Book` object, we could change it a little:

```
class Category
  include Mongoid::Document

  has_and_belongs_to_many :books, inverse_of: nil
end
```

Let see what happens when we execute the following commands:

```
irb> b = Book.new
 => #<Book _id: 4ef5ab79fed0eb89bf000002, _type: nil, title: nil,
publisher: "Dover Publications", category_ids = [], category_name:
"Oliver Twist">


irb> c = Category.last
 => #<Category _id: 4ef5b48efed0eb8d17000001, _type: nil, name: "Drama",
book_ids: []>


irb> c.books << b
 => [BSON::ObjectId('4ef5ab79fed0eb89bf000002')]


irb>  c
 => #<Category _id: 4ef5b48efed0eb8d17000001, _type: nil, name: "Drama",
book_ids: [BSON::ObjectId('4ef5ab79fed0eb89bf000002')]>


irb> b
 => #<Book _id: 4ef5ab79fed0eb89bf000002, _type: nil, title: nil,
publisher: "Dover Publications", category_ids = [], category_name:
"Oliver Twist">
```

Seems almost as similar to the earlier version. However, let's take a closer look:

```
irb>  c
 => #<Category _id: 4ef5b48efed0eb8d17000001, _type: nil, name: "Drama",
```

```
book_ids: [BSON::ObjectId('4ef5ab79fed0eb89bf000002')]>

irb> b
 => #<Book _id: 4ef5ab79fed0eb89bf000002, _type: nil, title: nil,
publisher: "Dover Publications",

category_ids = [],

category_name: "Oliver Twist">
```

Notice that the inverse relation was not set in the `Book` object. In other words, since the `inverse_of` object was `nil`, the array that should have contained the `ObjectId` instances of the categories is empty.

Remember that the `inverse_of` method is called from that model. The previous `category_ids` example will not be updated if the `Category` object is updated with books.

 If you update the books with categories, that is `b.categories << c`, then `category_ids` in the `Book` object will get populated!

Let's see if we can set up `following` and `followers` between authors. An author can follow other authors and be followed by other authors too!

```
    class Author
      include Mongoid::Document

      has_and_belongs_to_many :followers,
                                 class_name: "Author",
                                 inverse_of: :following

      has_and_belongs_to_many :following,
                class_name: "Author",
                inverse_of: :followers

    end
```

Let's set up some relationships between authors as follows:

```
irb> > a = Author.first
 => #<Author _id: 4e86e4b6fed0eb0be0000011, _type: nil, name: "Charles
Dickens", follower_ids: [], following_ids: []>


irb> > b = Author.last
```

```
=> #<Author _id: 4ef5ab6ffed0eb89bf000001, _type: nil, name: "Mark
Twain", follower_ids: [], following_ids: []>


irb> a.following << b

=> [BSON::ObjectId('4ef5ab6ffed0eb89bf000001')]


irb> a

=> #<Author _id: 4e86e4b6fed0eb0be0000011, _type: nil, name: "Charles
Dickens", follower_ids: [], following_ids: [BSON::ObjectId('4ef5ab6ffed0e
b89bf000001')]>


irb> b

=> #<Author _id: 4ef5ab6ffed0eb89bf000001, _type: nil, name: "Mark
Twain", follower_ids: [BSON::ObjectId('4e86e4b6fed0eb0be0000011')],
following_ids: []>


irb> a.following

=> [#<Author _id: 4ef5ab6ffed0eb89bf000001, _type: nil, name: "Mark
Twain", follower_ids: [BSON::ObjectId('4e86e4b6fed0eb0be0000011')],
following_ids: []>]


irb> b.followers

=> [#<Author _id: 4e86e4b6fed0eb0be0000011, _type: nil, name: "Charles
Dickens", follower_ids: [], following_ids: [BSON::ObjectId('4ef5ab6ffed0e
b89bf000001')]>]
```

Let's analyze the code carefully. What we wanted was `followers` and `following`
between authors. As an author can have many followers and can also follow many
authors, we set this up as a Many-to-Many relation. This is shown next:

```
class Author
  include Mongoid::Document

  has_and_belongs_to_many :followers,
                          class_name: "Author",
                          inverse_of: :following

  has_and_belongs_to_many :following,
        class_name: "Author",
        inverse_of: :followers
end
```

Note that it's the `Author` model that an author follows and can get followed. So, the class name is the same. This is also called a recursive relation.

```
class Author
  include Mongoid::Document

  has_and_belongs_to_many :followers,
                          class_name: "Author",
                          inverse_of: :following

  has_and_belongs_to_many :following,
      class_name: "Author",
      inverse_of: :followers
end
```

Now, we want to maintain different arrays for following and followers. So, whenever we define the follower relation, we need to update its counterpart or the inverse relation too. That is why the `:following` relation has `inverse_of` `:followers` and vice versa! This is shown clearly in the following code:

```
class Author
  include Mongoid::Document

  has_and_belongs_to_many :followers,
                          class_name: "Author",
                          inverse_of: :following

  has_and_belongs_to_many :following,
      class_name: "Author",
      inverse_of: :followers
end
```

Now, let's see the actual working of this relationship. When we set up the following for one author, we do it as follows:

```
irb> a.following << b
 => [BSON::ObjectId('4ef5ab6ffed0eb89bf000001')]
```

When this is done, we can see that the `follower_ids` object of `a` and the `following_ids` of `b` are updated together! This is shown in the following code:

```
irb> a.following
 => [#<Author _id: 4ef5ab6ffed0eb89bf000001, _type: nil, name: "Mark
Twain",
follower_ids: [BSON::ObjectId('4e86e4b6fed0eb0be0000011')],
```

```
following_ids: [] >]


irb> b.followers
 => [#<Author _id: 4e86e4b6fed0eb0be0000011, _type: nil, name: "Charles
Dickens",
follower_ids: [],
following_ids: [BSON::ObjectId('4ef5ab6ffed0eb89bf000001')]>]
```

Polymorphic relations

Polymorphic means multiple forms or multiple behaviors. For example, a vehicle could mean a two-wheeler, three-wheeler, a car, a truck, or even a space shuttle! So, how do we map these different types of vehicles that have entirely different data but have a relatively common functionality? Enter polymorphic relations! Let's create vehicles using basic polymorphism.

Let's design the Vehicle model:

```
# app/models/vehicle.rb

class Vehicle
  include Mongoid::Document

  belongs_to :resource, polymorphic: true

  field :terrain, type: String
  field :cost, type: Float
  field :weight, type: Float
  field :max_speed, type: Float
end
```

This is the main polymorphic class. We now use this class in other models. Now, each model we build is independent and can choose to be related to Vehicle. It has its own identity and does not inherit from any parent model, but it will be treated like a vehicle.

Let's create a Bike class:

```
# app/models/bike.rb
class Bike
  include Mongoid::Document

  has_one :vehicle, as: resource

  field :gears, type: Integer
```

```
      field :has_handle, type: Boolean
      field :cubic_capacity, type: Float
   end
```

And here is the entirely different `Ship` model as follows:

```
# app/models/ship.rb
class Ship
   include Mongoid::Document

   has_one :vehicle, as: resource

   field :is_military, type: Boolean
   field :is_cruise, type: Boolean
   field :missile_capable, type: Boolean
   field :anti_aircraft, type: Boolean
   field :number_engines, type: Integer
end
```

Here, you see that each model has properties that are totally different from each other but still they all fall under the `Vehicle` category. One of the advantages of polymorphism is that it's easy to enter and exit from this pattern. It's very easy to incorporate an existing model into a polymorphic pattern and equally easy to remove an existing model from it. We just add or remove the relationship to the polymorphic model.

Now let's build objects as follows:

```
irb> ship = Ship.new(is_military: true)


 => #<Ship _id: 4f042c53fed0ebc45b000003, _type: "Ship", is_military:
true, is_cruise: nil, missile_capable: nil, anti_aircraft: nil, number_
engines: nil>


irb> vehicle = Vehicle.create(resource: ship)


 => #<Vehicle _id: 4f042c87fed0ebc481000002, _type: "Vehicle", resource_
type: "Ship", resource_id: BSON::ObjectId('4f042c53fed0ebc45b000003'),
terrain: nil, cost: nil, weight: nil, max_speed: nil>
```

Notice the `resource_id` and `resource_type` fields, they define the resource that the vehicle represents.

embeds_many – embedding many documents

This method sets up the parent embedded relation for a single embedded child. All embedded documents are saved inside the parent document. So, when you fetch the parent document, all the embedded documents are also part of it. When we use `embeds_many`, the embedded documents are saved in an array inside the document. This is the most commonly used relation.

```
class Book
  include Mongoid::Document

  embeds_many :reviews
end
```

As embedded documents can be polymorphic, the `:as` option is supported along with the relation callbacks `:before_add`, `:after_add`, `:before_remove`, and `:after_remove`. will be discussed next.

:cascade_callbacks

As embedded documents are part of the parent, their callbacks are not automatically invoked when the parent is saved. We need to explicitly set this option if we want the embedded child document to process callbacks.

```
class Book
  include Mongoid::Document

  embeds_many :reviews, cascade_callbacks: true
end
```

:store_as

The `store_as` option allows the name of the embedded document to be changed.

:cyclic

The :cyclic option is used as an option for recursive or cyclic relationships. This method is very specific for embedded documents. This method is useful for setting up a hierarchy of embedded documents—a single parent and multiple embedded child documents. Let's set up some cyclic relations. We have seen how we can configure an author with following and followers using the inverse_of option. Now, let's build the Author class and its followers using cyclic relationships! This can be done as follows:

```
class Author
  include Mongoid::Document

  embeds_many :child_authors, class_name: "Author", cyclic: true
  embedded_in :parent_author, class_name: "Author", cyclic: true

end
```

And let's update the objects as follows:

```
irb> a = Author.first
 => #<Author _id: 4e86e4b6fed0eb0be0000011, _type: nil, name: "Charles
Dickens">


irb> a.child_authors << Author.last
 => true


irb> a.child_authors.first.parent_author
 => #<Author _id: 4ef5ab6ffed0eb89bf000001, _type: nil, name: "Mark
Twain">
```

We now embed an array called child_authors into the Author document, and then reference the parent using the parent_author field. We can also do the exact same thing we just saw using the following code:

```
class Author
  include Mongoid::Document

  recursively_embeds_many

end
```

embeds_one – embed one document

This relation takes the standard options, which we have seen earlier: `:autobuild`, `:as`, `:cascade_callbacks`, `:cyclic`, `:store_as`, and so on. However, it's interesting how we can manage relations using the names of the relations.

What if we want to save the relation twice in the same parent class? For example, in the `Author` model, we want the permanent and current addresses. Both are `Address` objects. We use the `name` option that specifies the name of the relation in which the information would be stored. Have a look at the following code:

```
class Author
  include Mongoid::Document

  embeds_one :permanent_address, class_name: "Address"
  embeds_one :current_address, class_name: "Address"
end

class Address
  include Mongoid::Document

  embedded_in :author, inverse_of: :permanent_address
  embedded_in :author, inverse_of: :current_address
end
```

If we create an author now, MongoDB stores both the addresses under different names:

```
{ "_id" : ObjectId("51b42d4245db7c9535000001"),
  "name" : "a4",
  "current_address" : { "_id" :
    ObjectId("51b42d4e45db7c9535000002"), "city" : "P"
  },
  "permanent_address" : { "_id" :
    ObjectId("51b42d5a45db7c9535000003"), "city" : "z"
  }
}
```

This is how we can embed the same object into the document under different names using the `:name` option.

embedded_in – resolving children

The `embedded_in` method tells us in which object this is embedded. It's very important that this should be configured when we are setting up the embedded relations.

 Without the `embedded_in` method in the model, the document would not get embedded at all. This is because the method is used to find the inverse relation!

```
class Review
  include Mongoid::Document

    embedded_in :book
end
```

This tells Mongoid that the review document is embedded inside the book.

Embedded polymorphic relations

As we must set the `embedded_in` relation between the parent and the child, how do we embed the same document in different objects? Make it polymorphic! We have seen some examples of writing polymorphic relations earlier, and they can be used exactly like that even in embedded documents.

Summary

In this chapter, we saw how we can manipulate relations between documents. We saw all the basic relations with their various configuration options. We also saw some complex cases of cyclic relations and polymorphic relations.

In the next chapter, we shall study how to query documents and their related documents.

5
Mongoid Queries

In this chapter, we will learn everything about querying documents. We will see how to fire queries on various data types, embedded documents, and indexed queries. We will learn about criteria, lazy evaluation, and eager loading! We will also take a quick look at aggregations and MapReduce.

Mongoid querying DSL (domain-specific language or grammar) has been abstracted into a gem called Origin. This gem provides ActiveRelation styles to Mongoid queries. Origin can be used on its own, even without Mongoid and the main reason for this was to write a generic querying DSL that can be used independently.

Origins of Origin

Origin is just an extraction of Mongoid's criteria into its own gem. In the extraction, I rewrote most of it since over the last 3 years the criteria had gotten some unsavory code in it. With the rewrite, I was able to add more functionality to it, like alias handling, better attribute serialization, the ability to pass any object with a proper serializer (like a document itself), and custom merge strategies. Plus it has the bonus that anyone who wants to leverage the API can use it, and doesn't have to be using Mongoid. It supports every single possible query operation MongoDB can do, and would be quite useful in other gems that don't necessarily need a full-blown data mapper, but would like the DSL – Durran Jordan, author of Mongoid gem.

This was in March 2012! The thoughts have indeed been noble! Origin has since then evolved tremendously but still boasts of being an independent entity. Origin is not a data mapper but a querying Domain-Specific Language (DSL). What makes Origin more likable is that it adheres to the `ActiveRelation` syntax. That means we can now use queries such as `where`, `count`, and `distinct`.

Origin standardizes the querying process. It also adds support for some data types that are not supported in MongoDB. For example, MongoDB does not have a `BigDecimal` data type but Origin does! We have seen what custom serialization is in the earlier chapters. The following is how a `BigDecimal` data type is saved in MongoDB.

```
def evolve(object)
  __evolve__(object) do |obj|
    obj ? obj.to_s : obj
  end
end
```

As we can see, it's stored as a string and serialized into a `BigDecimal` data type when loaded. Similarly, it's well known that MongoDB saves all date and time in UTC. So, Origin takes care of marshaling and un-marshaling this data for us.

 Origin can even save the range and symbol objects in MongoDB!

There are a lot of new convenient and useful routines that have been introduced because of Origin. For example, `:between` and `:and` and `:or`.

Query selectors

The following is a list of all supported methods that are supported on any Mongoid class. The following table states the attributes of the query selectors, their usage, and description:

`:all`	`Book.all(reviews: ['good', 'excellent'])`	This finds all the documents where the field (typically an array) matches all the values in the array. So, this means that `reviews` is an array inside the `Book` document, and it must contain at least two values `good` and `excellent`.
		In case `reviews` is an embedded document, we can also write this like the following code:
		`Book.all("reviews.content" => ['good', 'excellent'])`
`:exists`	`Author.exists(books_count: true)`	This finds all the documents in which the field exists.

:gt/:gte/:lt/:lte	Author.gt(books_count: 1) Author.lte(books_count: 10)	This finds all the documents in which count is greater than (:gt) or greater than or equal to (:gte) and lesser than (:lt) and lesser than or equal to (:lte).
:in :nin	Author.in(name: ['Gautam', 'Charles']) Book.nin(title: ['Draculla', 'Dr. Jekyll'])	This finds all the documents in which the field is in (:in) or not in (:nin) the array.
:elem_match	Book.elem_match(reviews: {content: 'good'})	This finds all the documents, which contain arrays, hashes, or embedded documents that we want to test the fields inside them. This is not a very frequently used operator. Alternatively, you can also do this: Book.where("reviews.content" => 'good').

We know that MongoDB supports geospatial searches. Mongoid leverages all the geospatial searches too with the symbol operators. The following table states the attributes of the operators, their usage, and description:

:near :near_sphere	Author.near('address.location' => [54, -123])	This finds all the documents that are near a particular geolocation. geospatial queries do not work unless the field is indexed as "2D".
:within_box	Author.within_box(location: [54, 60], [60, 70])	This finds all the documents that are within the geolocation box.
:within_circle :within_spherical_circle	Author.within_circle(location: [54, 60], 0.5)	This finds all the documents that are within a geolocation circle. The second parameter is the radius.
:within_polygon	Author.within_polygon(location: [10, 20], [10, 40], [30, 40], [30, 20])	This finds all the documents that are within a geolocation polygon.

Overloading the Symbol class

When the Mongoid gem is loaded, a lot of the selector methods we saw earlier are also overloaded on the `Symbol` class. We have an alternate syntax for querying on symbols. For example:

```
Book.where(:published_date.lte => Date.today)
```

This helps us add custom selectors and is easier to write than something like the following:

```
Book.where(:published_date => { "$lte" => Date.today })
```

It's important to remember that symbol operators work only on the fields in the document and not on the relations.

A word of caution: Overloading methods on the `Symbol` class can be dangerous if there is more than one library injecting customizations on the `Symbol` class. It's recommended to use the standard built-in methods on the class.

Mongoid criteria

The `Mongoid::Criteria` module is the core object for querying MongoDB. This includes the entire Origin DSL for querying along with other goodies. Every time a query is fired, a criterion is created. For example, in the following query, we do not get back a result but a criterion object:

```
irb> Book.exists(awards: true)
 => #<Mongoid::Criteria
  selector:  {"awards"=>{"$exists"=>true}}
  options:   {}
  class:     Book
  embedded:  false>
```

This criterion can now be chained with other criteria, just like `ActiveRelation`. This helps us fire a single query to the database only when all the criteria are fully resolved:

```
> Book.exists(awards: true).count
 => 20
```

In addition to the methods provided in Origin, some helpful criteria are mentioned as follows:

`:count`
`:length`
`:size`
	`Author.count`
	`Author.where(name: 'Charles').`
	`length`
	`Author.where(name: 'Charles').`
	`size`
		This finds the number of documents in the collection.

`:distinct` `:pluck`	`Author.distinct(:name)` `Author.pluck(:name)`	This returns an array of all the distinct fields in the collection. Remember that this does not return the object, but the distinct fields from all the documents in that collection! The `pluck` object returns all the non-nil fields. So, if there are any Author objects without a name, it will be ignored.
`:each` `:exists?`	`Author.each { |a| p a.name }` `Author.exists?(name: "Charles")`	The `:each` object iterates over each document and executes the block while `:exists?` checks if there is at least one document that meets the criteria.

`:find`
`:find_by`
`:find_or_`
`create_by`
`:find_or_`
`initialize_`
`by`
	`Author.`
	`find("5143678345db7ca255000001")`
	`Author.find_by(name: "Charles")`
	`Author.find_or_create_by(name:`
	`"Charles")`
	`Author.find_or_initialize_`
	`by(name:`
	`"Charles")`
		This finds the document by ID (by default) or by the criteria passed to `find_by`. We can create or instantiate an object by calling the `find_or_create_by` and `find_or_initialize_by` view, respectively.

`:first`
`:last`
`:first_or_`
`create`
`:first_or_`
`create!`
`:first_or_`
`initialize`
	`Author.first`
	`Author.first_or_create(name:`
	`"Charles")`
	`Author.first_or_create!(name:`
	`"Charles")`
	`Author.first_or_`
	`initialize(name: "Charles")`
		This finds the first or last document by default or by the criteria passed to it. We can create or instantiate the first object by calling the `first_or_create` and `first_or_initialize` functions, respectively. As always the bang method raises an exception if the validation fails.

As we have seen earlier, querying attributes is very easy in Mongoid. We can fire queries just like in the following code snippet:

```
> Author.where(name: 'Gautam')

=> #<Mongoid::Criteria
  selector: {"name"=>"Gautam"}
  options:  {}
  class:    Author
  embedded: false>
```

This is the Mongoid criterion. The data is not returned until required. To access the data, we need to fire the `collect` operation or the first action as follows:

```
> Author.where(name: 'Gautam').first
=> #<Author _id: 515085fd45db7c911e000003, name: "Gautam",
  last_name: nil, wallet: nil, password: nil>
```

Queries on arrays and hashes

We can easily search in arrays and hashes as we did with fields. For example, if a `Book` class has `awards`, we can search in the `awards` field. Let's see some code regarding the same:

```
irb> b = Book.first
 => #<Book _id: 516e7ab045db7cd86a000001, t(title): "Aristortle",
... published_date: nil, is_best_seller: false, awards: [], currency:
nil>

irb> b.awards
 => []

irb> b.awards << 'first place'
 => ["first place"]

irb> b.awards << 'second place'
 => ["first place", "second place"]

irb> b.awards << 'third place'
 => ["first place", "second place", "third place"]

irb> b.save
 => true
```

Now, we can search in the `awards` fields in the usual way as follows:

```
irb> Book.in(awards: ['second place']).first
```

```
=> #<Book _id: 516e7ab045db7cd86a000001, t(title): "Aristortle",
   published_date: nil, is_best_seller: false, awards: ["first
   place", "second place", "third place"], currency: nil>
```

However, searching inside an array could also be done in the following way:

```
> Book.where(awards: 'second place').first
```

```
=> #<Book _id: 516e7ab045db7cd86a000001, t(title): "Aristortle",
   published_date: nil, is_best_seller: false, awards: ["first
   place", "second place", "third place"], currency: nil>
```

So far so good. What if we have an array of hashes or better, still an array of embedded documents! It's still the same! Let's see some examples, a book has reviews, which are embedded documents! Let's add a few reviews to a book first using the following code:

```
irb> b = Book.all.sample
=> #<Book _id: 51b75aaf45db7cc8b4000001, t(title): "How to deal?",
   ... author_id: BSON::ObjectId('5143678345db7ca255000001')>
```

```
irb> b.reviews << Review.new(content: 'awesome')
 => [#<Review _id: 527aa81433352d01f0000000, content: "awesome">]
```

```
irb> b.reviews << Review.new(content: 'sucks!')
 => [#<Review _id: 527aa81433352d01f0000000, content: "awesome">,
  #<Review _id: 527aa81a33352d01f0010000, content: "sucks!">]
```

Now, if we want to search inside an array of hashes or embedded documents, we can fire the query as follows:

```
> Book.where('reviews.content' => /awesome/).first
=> #<Book _id: 51b75aaf45db7cc8b4000001, t(title): "How to deal?",
   ,,, author_id: BSON::ObjectId('5143678345db7ca255000001')>
```

As we can see, searching inside the array of hashes (or embedded documents) can work with the dot notation too!

Scopes

Mongoid uses the ActiveModel scopes, for instance:

```ruby
class Book
  include Mongoid::Document

  field :t, as: :title, type: String
  field :published_date, type: Date
  field :is_best_seller, type: Boolean, default: false
  field :awards, type: Array, default: []
  field :reviews, type: Hash

  scope :latest, gte(published_date: Date.parse('2013/1/1'))
end
```

This scope can be used as:

```ruby
Book.latest
```

This will effectively fire the following query:

```ruby
Book.gte(published_date: Date.parse('2013/1/1')
```

Now, let's see some interesting Ruby code. We now want to write some generic scope for "the books in the current year and not just 2013". That should be simple enough.

```ruby
scope :latest, gte(published_date: Date.today.beginning_of_year)
```

Surprise, surprise! This will work fine for the current year but next year (assuming the server has not been restarted) this will fail! This is because the scope is resolved when the class is loaded. Let's see a more practical example of this mistake!

```ruby
scope :latest, gte(published_date: (Date.today -
  rand(10).years).beginning_of_year)
```

So, now we are not sure of the year that will be set. However, you will notice that a randomized value gets set only once!

The correct code for this scope is as follows:

```ruby
scope :latest, -> { gte(published_date: Date.today.beginning_of_year)
}
```

The scope function can take a `Proc` object, and it gets executed whenever the scope is invoked. This will cater to even the following years.

The syntax `-> { #some code here }` is called a **stabby** lambda and is available from Ruby 1.9 onwards. Rails4 now requires a callable object like a lambda for managing scopes.

Atomic modifiers

Atomic modifiers are those that modify the fields in an atomic operation. We saw an example of this in the earlier chapter with `:counter_cache`, which atomically increments or decrements the value of a field.

While it's easy to manipulate fields in a document, how about if we want to atomically find or modify documents? In SQL, we have `INSERT ON DUPLICATE KEY UPDATE` and this is called an upsert. Similarly, MongoDB also supports upserts. We have already seen methods, such as `:find_and_create` and `:find_and_initialize`. Now, we will see `:find_and_modify`.

find_and_modify

As the name suggests, we find and modify in a single atomic operation. This is useful in various scenarios where we want to *compare and set* in a single operation. For example, a `Job` queue, where a worker processes is supposed to pick up a job and execute them. It's important that only one worker picks up a job. Suppose we have a job class as follows:

```
class Job
  include Mongoid::Document

  field :name
  field :status, type: Boolean, default: false
end
```

Now, if we have workers' processes, they need to pick up a job which shows `status: false` and helps them to execute it. However, if we were to implement this in the following way, we may have trouble:

```
irb> j = Job.where(status: false).first
=> => #<Job _id: 51df929245db7cb313000002, name: 0, status: false>

irb> j.status = true
true

irb> j.save
=> => #<Job _id: 51df929245db7cb313000002, name: 0, status: true>
```

This is fine as long as there is only one worker. Now, if there were more than one worker processes doing this, it could lead to trouble.

```
WORKER 1 irb> j = Job.where(status: false).first
=> #<Job _id: 51df929245db7cb313000002, name: 0, status: false>


WORKER 1 irb> j.status = true
true


WORKER 2 irb> j = Job.where(status: false).first
=> #<Job _id: 51df929245db7cb313000002, name: 0, status: false>


WORKER 1 irb> j.save
=> => #<Job _id: 51df929245db7cb313000002, name: 0, status: true>


WORKER 2 irb> j.status = true
true


WORKER 2 irb> j.save
=> => #<Job _id: 51df929245db7cb313000002, name: 0, status: true>
```

As we can see, both worker processes now think they own the same job! To avoid this, we use `:find_and_modify`, to ensure that the lookup and the update happen in one atomic operation.

```
irb> j = Job.where(status: false).find_and_modify({ '$set' => { status:
true} }, new: true)
=> #<Job _id: 51df929245db7cb31300000b, name: 9, status: true>
```

This is now guaranteed to be atomic as only one command was fired. For the inquisitive, this was the MongoDB command that got fired:

```
[conn208] command sodibee_development.$cmd command: { findAndModify:
"jobs", query: { status: false }, new: true, update: { $set: { status:
true } } } update: { $set: { status: true } } ntoreturn:1 idhack:1
nupdated:1 fastmod:1 keyUpdates:0 locks(micros) w:245 reslen:132 0ms
```

 Remember, unlike criteria, a `find_and_modify` operation gets executed immediately!

Querying with indexed fields

Indexing increases the query performance tremendously but causes some overheads in write operations. We will learn in great detail about the various types of indexes in the next chapter. When we index fields, it's important to maintain the right order. For example, for the `Book` model, if we will always search by the title, and then maybe by the author and published date, it makes sense to create a compound index.

```
class Book
  ...

  index({title: 1, author: 1, published_date: 1}
end
```

So, if we now try to search for books and the title is present, it will always use the `BTreeCursor` indexed search that is faster. However, if the title is not used in searches, the `BasicCursor` function is relatively slower.

 `BTreeCursor`, as the name suggests, uses a **Binary Tree** for storing the index. This will change our index searches complexity to $O(log2n)$, where *n* is the number of values that are indexed. When no index is specified on the field, the search is linear $O(n)$. By default `_id` that is, the object ID, is always indexed.

Covered queries

Covered queries are those queries where MongoDB does not look at documents, but only at the index. If we select only the fields that are indexed, the query gets covered. For example:

```
irb> Book.only(title: 1).where(title: /count/)
```

In this query, we want only the title and since the title is indexed, this gets fired *only* for the index and not the document. The decision to look only in the index resides with MongoDB and its internal logic. To check if the query will be fired using the index only, use `:explain`. For instance, see the following code example:

```
irb> Book.only(title: 1).where(title: /count/).explain
{
  "cursor" : "BtreeCursor t_1_author_id_1_published_date_1 multi",
  "isMultiKey" : false,
  "n" : 1,
  "nscannedObjects" : 1,
  "nscanned" : 11,
  "nscannedObjectsAllPlans" : 1,
```

```
    "nscannedAllPlans" : 11,
    "scanAndOrder" : false,
    "indexOnly" : true,
    "nYields" : 0,
    "nChunkSkips" : 0,
    "millis" : 0,
    "indexBounds" : {
        ...
    }
}
```

The aggregation framework

The aggregation framework of MongoDB was introduced from MongoDB v2.0. It gives us similar functionality, such as the GROUP BY in SQL. This could be achieved easily by using MapReduce, but the aggregation is simpler!

Mongoid currently provides only the following basic aggregations: :count, :min, :max, :sum, and :avg.

So, to get a count of all the books use the following code:

```
irb> Book.count
=> 12

irb> Book.avg(:reviews_count)
 => 1.3333333333333333
```

The aggregation framework will be discussed in detail in the next chapter. In short, it uses an pipeline that streams output from one operation as the input of the next operation in the pipeline (similar to the | operator on the Unix shell). Though Mongoid supports the basic aggregations, we can also define our own complex aggregation pipelines. However, the aggregate method is not directly available on the models (as yet). Instead, we need to invoke it on the collection. Let's see an example that shows how we can get the aggregation of all the author names and their book counts!

```
> Author.collection.aggregate({ "$group" => { "_id" => "$name",
  count: { "$sum" => "$books_count" } } })


=> [{"_id"=>"Charles", "count"=>1}, {"_id"=>"a2", "count"=>0},
  {"_id"=>"a1", "count"=>0}, {"_id"=>"Gautam Rege", "count"=>0},
  {"_id"=>"after1", "count"=>0}, {"_id"=>"Gautam", "count"=>0},
  {"_id"=>"Gautam Rege4", "count"=>0}, {"_id"=>"a4", "count"=>2},
  {"_id"=>"a3", "count"=>0}, {"_id"=>"Nested Author", "count"=>0},
```

```
{"_id"=>"AFTER ADD", "count"=>0}, {"_id"=>"Gautam Rege2",
"count"=>0}, {"_id"=>"Nested Author1", "count"=>0}]
```

This is way faster than doing this in Ruby:

```
> Author.all.collect {|c| [c.name, c.books.count] }
```

Notice that we are using $name and $books_count. This is a quick mapping of what aggregations are supported.

Refer to `http://docs.mongodb.org/manual/reference/sql-aggregation-comparison/` for further information.

$sum	`mongo> db.orders.aggregate( [ { $group: { _id: null, count: { $sum: 1 } } } ] )` For SQL use following: `SELECT COUNT(*) AS count FROM orders`	This is equivalent to the SUM or COUNT in SQL. This will get the count of all the orders.
$match	`db.orders.aggregate( [ { $group: { _id: "$cust_id", count: { $sum: 1 } } }, { $match: { count: { $gt: 1 } } } ] )` For SQL use following: `SELECT cust_id, count(*) FROM orders GROUP BY cust_id HAVING count(*) > 1`	This is equivalent to the WHERE or HAVING conditions in SQL along with a GROUP BY query.

In addition to these, we can also use $sort and $project for sorting and field selection in an aggregation.

 The $unwind operator is pretty useful. It peels of elements in an Array and returns them a stream of documents instead. This is very useful if we need to manipulate the data in the pipeline. We shall learn about this in later chapters.

Geolocation queries

Geolocation is in-built into MongoDB, and is one of its distinguishing features. We have seen examples of 2d or 2dsphere index in earlier chapters, and also seen how we can use the near criterion. Using $geoNear, that is, the geo_near method we can get geospatial criteria easily.

One of the common problems in geospatial search is that the queries use radians and not distance units (kilometers, or miles). MongoDB provides a distanceMultiplier operator that we can use to ensure consistency.

So, this query will give results with the distance in miles:

```
Author.geo_near([ 50, 13 ]).distance_multiplier(3959)
```

 The earth has a radius of approximately 3,959 miles or 6,371 km.

Suppose, we find all authors within a 10 miles radius of [34.052923, -84.44399]. First and foremost, when using only latitude and longitude, using a 2dsphere index is recommended. So, let's modify the Author model.

```
class Address
  include Mongoid::Document
  ...

  field :location, type: Array  # the location co-ordinates
end

class Author
  include Mongoid::Document
  ...

  index({'address.location' => '2dsphere', { min: 180, max: -180 })
end
```

Now, let's see how to fire the actual queries.

 When using 2dsphere, it's imperative to fire a spherical query for geo_near.

```
irb> Author.geo_near([34.052923,-84.44399])
        .spherical.max_distance(10.0 / 3959)
```

This fires a spherical `geo_near` query within a radius of 10 miles. Notice, the code `max_distance(10.0 / 3959)`, this is to convert the distance into radians. And since we want 10 miles, we convert miles into radians.

 The `:max_distance` operation also serves one more interesting purpose. If it is passed a parameter, it will scope the search within that distance. If it is invoked without parameters, it will display the distance of the most distant document!

```
irb> Author.geo_near([34.052923,-84.44399])
        .spherical.max_distance
=> 0.00710546708072593
```

This result is in radians. Since we want it in miles, we need to use a distance multiplier as follows:

```
irb> Author.geo_near([34.052923,-84.44399])
        .spherical.max_distance.distance_multiplier(3959)
=> 28.130544172593957
```

Ah! Now, this makes more sense. The most distant document is 28.1 miles away!

Summary

Now, you should be well versed with how to query documents from Mongoid. We learned some interesting concepts about aggregation in MongoDB too! We saw how Origin is used to make Mongoid a better querying framework. There's still a long way to go.

In the next chapters, we will see how to improve our performance using Indexes and also how to tune MongoDB. We will also learn more about the aggregation framework and MapReduce!

This is a spherical geometry, users query within a radius of 10 miles. Notice the radius max distance is 0... 1865... basis to convert the distance into radians. And since we want 10 miles, we convert miles into radians...

6
Performance Tuning

After understanding the basic concepts of documents, relations between documents, and how to query them, it's now time to see how we can improve the performance of Mongoid and MongoDB.

Though MongoDB is already known for its fast reads and writes, it's important to set it up and configure it properly. After that, it's important to set the right indexes for the data we have. Finally, it's important to monitor slow queries and optimize them.

MongoDB environment

MongoDB works on all common operating systems, but it is frequently used in production with Enterprise Linux on 64-bit systems. Do remember that MongoDB uses memory-mapped files for speed and all indexes are stored in memory. So, MongoDB can indeed consume quite a lot of memory.

Typically, if you have a server that has 4 GB to 8 GB memory and a dual or quad core CPU, it's a good start. Disk space is never a concern in today's world; so, the more the disk space the better it is.

MongoDB automatically gets all the benefits of VM improvements. So, as the page fault management improves, MongoDB performance "automagically" improves!

If you are using a Linux system, it's highly recommended that the filesystem should be ext4 or XFS formatted and the kernel Version should be 2.6.36 or later.

 Some commands mentioned here are specific to Ubuntu. If you are on a different operating system, use the relevant command.

To format the /data partition as ext4 on Ubuntu, issue the following command:

```
$ sudo mke2fs -t ext4 /data
```

Along with this, you should also ensure that there is enough swap space too. On Ubuntu, create a swap space of 2 GB and enable it as follows:

```
$ sudo dd if=/dev/zero of=/swapfile bs=1M count=2048
$ sudo mkswap /swapfile
$ sudo swapon /swapfile
```

Indexes

Indexing ensures faster reads. However, indexes have a hit on writes, that is, creation and updating of documents. There are various types of indexes supported by MongoDB. We have already seen these various types of indexes earlier.

Indexes are not automatically created. When we specify the index in our model, we need to run the rake db:mongoid:create_ indexes command to create them. To get a list of database tasks that Mongoid supports, issue the rake -T db:mongoid command.

The following table gives a quick summary of the various options that are available for index creation:

Name	Example	Description
normal	index({name: 1}) index({name: 1}, {name: 'n'}) index({"address.location" => 1})	This is the typical index that gets created. The index name gets saved as a concatenation of the field names unless the :name option is provided. Also, notice that indexes can be ordered in ascending or descending order using 1 and -1, respectively.
unique drop_dups	index({name: 1}, { unique: true}) index({name: 1}, { unique: true, drop_dups: true})	This ensures that the index is unique. drop_dups forces creation of unique indexes.
background	index({name: 1}, { unique: true, background: true})	The background option creates indexes asynchronously, so that it does not impact application performance.

Write concern

MongoDB helps us ensure write consistency. This means that when we write something to MongoDB, it now guarantees the success of the write operation. Interestingly, this is a configurable option and is set to acknowledged by default. This means that the write is guaranteed because it waits for an acknowledgement before returning success.

In earlier versions of Mongoid, `safe: true` was turned off by default. This meant that success of the write operation was not guaranteed. The write concern is configured in `Mongoid.yml` as follows:

```
development:
  sessions:
    default:
      hosts:
        - localhost:27017
      options:
        write:
          w: 1
```

The default write concern in Mongoid is configured with `w: 1`, which means that the success of a write operation is guaranteed. Let's see an example:

```
class Author
  include Mongoid::Document

  field :name, type: String

  index( {name: 1}, {unique: true, background: true})

end
```

 Indexing blocks read and write operations. Hence, its recommended to configure indexing in the background in a Rails application.

We shall now start a Rails console and see how this reacts to a duplicate key index by creating two `Author` objects with the same name.

```
irb> Author.create(name: "Gautam")
=> #<Author _id: 5143678345db7ca255000001, name: "Gautam">
```

```
irb> Author.create(name: "Gautam")

Moped::Errors::OperationFailure: The operation:
#<Moped::Protocol::Command
    @length=83
    @request_id=3
    @response_to=0
    @op_code=2004
    @flags=[]
    @full_collection_name="sodibee_development.$cmd"
    @skip=0
    @limit=-1
    @selector={:getlasterror=>1, :w=>1}
    @fields=nil>
failed with error 11000: "E11000 duplicate key error index: sodibee_
development.authors.$name_1  dup key: { : \"Gautam\" }"
```

As we can see, it has raised a `duplicate key error` and the document is not saved.
Now, let's have some fun. Let's change the write concern to unacknowledged:

```
development:
  sessions:
    default:
      hosts:
        - localhost:27017
      options:
        write:
          w: 0
```

The write concern is now set to unacknowledged writes. That means we do not wait
for the MongoDB write to eventually succeed, but assume that it will. Now let's see
what happens with the same command that had failed earlier.

```
irb > Author.where(name: "Gautam").count
 => 1

irb > Author.create(name: "Gautam")
 => #<Author _id: 5287cba54761755624000000, name: "Gautam">

irb > Author.where(name: "Gautam").count
 => 1
```

There seems to be a discrepancy here. Though Mongoid `create` returned successfully, the data was not saved to the database. Since we specified `background: true` for the `name` index, the document creation seemed to succeed as MongoDB had not indexed it yet, and we did not wait for acknowledging the success of the write operation. So, when MongoDB tries to index the data in the background, it realizes that the index criterion is not met (since the index is unique), and it deletes the document from the database. Now, since that was in the background, there is no way to figure this out on the console or in our Rails application. This leads to an inconsistent result.

So, how can we solve this problem? There are various ways to solve this problem:

- We leave the Mongoid default *write concern* configuration alone. By default, it is `w: 1` and it will raise an exception. This is the recommended approach as prevention is better than cure!

- Do not specify the `background: true` option. This will create indexes in the foreground. However, this approach is not recommended as it can cause a drop in performance because index creations block read and write access.

- Add `drop_dups: true`. This deletes data, so you have to be really careful when using this option.

Other options to the `index` command create different types of indexes as shown in the following table:

Index type	Example	Description
sparse	`index({twitter_name: 1}, { sparse: true})`	This creates sparse indexes, that is, only the documents containing the indexed fields are indexed. Use this with care as you can get incomplete results.
2d **2dsphere**	`index({:location => "2dsphere"})`	This creates a two-dimensional spherical index. We have seen this being used in the earlier chapters.

Compound index

We saw this briefly in the earlier chapters. When we index on multiple fields, the index is called a **compound index**.

```
class Book
  include Mongoid::Document

  field :title, type: String
  field :published_date, type: String
```

```
    belongs_to :author

    index({ title: 1, published_date: 1, author: 1})
  end
```

This creates a compound index for :title. When we query using the title field, it will always search in the index.

 MongoDB limits compound indexes to a maximum of 31 fields. This is more than enough in most cases.

The order of compound key indexing is critically important. In the preceding case, we have the compound index in this order: { title: 1, published_date: 1, author: 1}. Now, if we search for any query that has :title in it, it will use the binary search for getting faster results. However, if we search without :title in it, it will use the BasicCursor function and not the BinaryCursor function. Let's take a quick look at an example:

```
> db.books.find({title: /count/, author: /Charles/}).explain() {
  "cursor" : "BtreeCursor t_1_author_id_1_published_date_1 multi",
  "isMultiKey" : false,
  "n" : 0,
  "nscannedObjects" : 0,
  "nscanned" : 11,
  "nscannedObjectsAllPlans" : 11,
  "nscannedAllPlans" : 22,
  "scanAndOrder" : false,
  "indexOnly" : false,
  "nYields" : 0,
  "nChunkSkips" : 0,
  "millis" : 0,
  "indexBounds" : {
      ...
  },
  "server" : "Gautams-MacBook-Pro.local:27017"
}
```

However, if we fire the same query with `author` and `published_date` without the `title` field, it's the `BasicCursor` function that gets used.

```
> db.books.find({published_date: new Date,
  author: /Charles/}).explain() {
  "cursor" : "BasicCursor",
  "isMultiKey" : false,
  "n" : 0,
  "nscannedObjects" : 12,
  "nscanned" : 12,
  "nscannedObjectsAllPlans" : 12,
  "nscannedAllPlans" : 12,
  "scanAndOrder" : false,
  "indexOnly" : false,
  "nYields" : 0,
  "nChunkSkips" : 0,
  "millis" : 252,
  "indexBounds" : {

  },
  "server" : "Gautams-MacBook-Pro.local:27017"
}
```

It's very important to know the most common key in a compound index and *that key should be mentioned first when creating the index.*

However, when preparing the query, as long as the key is mentioned in any order, the `BtreeCursor` function will be invoked.

When you are using geospatial indexes in a compound key, the geo-spatial index *must* be mentioned first. For example:

```
index({ "address.location" => "2dsphere", 'address.city' => 1 },
   { min: -180, max: 180 })
```

Multikey index

Can we index on an array? Yes!

```
class Book
  include Mongoid::Document

  field :tags, type: Array

  index({tags: 1})
end
```

Now, MongoDB will create an index for each value of tags. We can also create a compound index with a **multikey** index. However, the restriction is that there can be only one multikey index in a compound index.

```
> db.books.find({tags: {$in: ['one']}}).explain() {
  "cursor" : "BtreeCursor tags_1",
  "isMultiKey" : true,
  "n" : 1,
  "nscannedObjects" : 1,
  "nscanned" : 1,
  "nscannedObjectsAllPlans" : 1,
  "nscannedAllPlans" : 1,
  "scanAndOrder" : false,
  "indexOnly" : false,
  "nYields" : 0,
  "nChunkSkips" : 0,
  "millis" : 0,
  "indexBounds" : {
    "tags" : [
      [
        "one",
        "one"
      ]
    ]
  },
  "server" : "Gautams-MacBook-Pro.local:27017"
}
>
```

If we want to see the criteria from the Rails console, we can issue the following command:

```
> Book.where(:tags.in => ['one'])
 => #<Mongoid::Criteria
  selector:  {"tags"=>{"$in"=>["one"]}}
  options:   {}
  class:     Book
  embedded:  false>
```

Hashed index

The default indexing mechanism is a Binary Tree. However, since v2.4, MongoDB supports a **hashed index** as well. The hashing function collapses the document and subdocuments into a hash that is used for lookups.

Needless to say, hashed indexes cannot support multikey indexes because the values are unknown at the time of indexing. The hash stored in the hashed index is 64 bits of the 128-bit md5 hash. Similarly, a hashed index does not support a range query because it cannot identity a hash for the range.

So, when should you use the hashed index?

Hashed index lookups are very fast — in technical terms O(1), that is, it's a direct lookup. B-tree index lookups are O(), which would be slightly slower.

However, a hashed index has limitations about multikey indexing and hashed indexes tend to manipulate floats for the hashing algorithm. So, they have data limitations. It should be noted that hashed indexes require more storage space than B-tree indexes. More information on this can be found at http://www.quora.com/Why-doesnt-mongodb-support-hash-indexes.

Text index

MongoDB 2.4 introduced **text indexes** that are as close to free text search indexes as it gets. However, it does only basic text indexing — that is, it supports stop words and stemming. It also assigns a relevance score with each search.

 Text indexes are still an experimental feature in MongoDB, and they are not recommended for extensive use. Use ElasticSearch, Solr (Sunspot), or ThinkingSphinx instead.

The following code snippet shows how we can specify a text index with weightage:

```
index({  "name" => 'text',
         "last_name" => 'text'
      },
      {
        weights: {
          'name' => 10,
          'last_name' => 5,
        },
        name: 'author_text_index'
      }
)
```

There is no direct search support in Mongoid (as yet). So, if you want to invoke a text search, you need to hack around a little.

```
irb> srch = Mongoid::Contextual::TextSearch.new(Author.collection,
Author.all, 'john')
 => #<Mongoid::Contextual::TextSearch
  selector:    {}
  class:       Author
  search:      john
  filter:      {}
  project:     N/A
  limit:       N/A
  language:    default>


irb> srch.execute
 => {"queryDebugString"=>"john||||||", "language"=>"english",
"results"=>[{"score"=>7.5, "obj"=>{"_id"=>BSON::ObjectId('51fc058345d
b7c843f00030b'), "name"=>"Bettye Johns"}}, {"score"=>7.5, "obj"=>{"_id
"=>BSON::ObjectId('51fc058345db7c843f00046d'), "name"=>"John Pagac"}},
{"score"=>7.5, "obj"=>{"_id"=>BSON::ObjectId('51fc058345db7c843f000578'),
"name"=>"Jeanie Johns"}}, {"score"=>7.5, "obj"=>{"_id"=>BSON::ObjectId('5
1fc058445db7c843f0007e7')

...

{"score"=>7.5, "obj"=>{"_id"=>BSON::ObjectId('51fc058a45db7c843
f0025f1'), "name"=>"Alford Johns"}}], "stats"=>{"nscanned"=>25,
"nscannedObjects"=>0, "n"=>25, "nfound"=>25, "timeMicros"=>31103},
"ok"=>1.0}
```

By default, text search is disabled in MongoDB configuration. We need to turn it on by adding `setParameter = textSearchEnabled=true` in the MongoDB configuration file, typically `/usr/local/mongo.conf`.

This returns a result with statistical data as well the documents and their relevance score. Interestingly, it also specifies the language. There are a few more things we can do with the search result. For example, we can see the statistical information as follows:

```
irb> a.stats
 => {"nscanned"=>25, "nscannedObjects"=>0, "n"=>25, "nfound"=>25,
"timeMicros"=>31103}
```

We can also convert the data into our Mongoid model objects by using `project`, as shown in the following command:

```
> a.project(:name).to_a
 => [#<Author _id: 51fc058345db7c843f00030b, name: "Bettye Johns",
last_name: nil, password: nil>, #<Author _id: 51fc058345db7c843f00046d,
name: "John Pagac", last_name: nil, password: nil>, #<Author _id:
51fc058345db7c843f000578, name: "Jeanie Johns", last_name: nil, password:
nil> ... ]
```

Some of the important things to remember are as follows:

- Text indexes can be very heavy in memory.
- They can return the documents, so the result can be large.
- We can use multiple keys (or filters) along with a text search. For example, the index with `index({ 'state': 1, name: 'text'})` will mandate the use of the state for every text search that is specified.
- A search for `"john doe"` will result in a search for `"john"` or `"doe"` or both.
- A search for `\"john\"` and `\"doe\"` will search for all `"john"` and `"doe"` in a random order.
- A search for `"\"john doe\""`, that is, with escaped quotes, will search for documents containing the exact phrase `"john doe"`.

A lot more data can be found at `http://docs.mongodb.org/manual/tutorial/search-for-text/`.

IdentityMap

This section is relevant only if you are using Mongoid 3. `IdentityMap` has been removed in Mongoid 4 because it now includes `Mongoid::Relations::Eager`.

An `IdentityMap` pattern is a design pattern where the object gets loaded only once from the database, and is then stored in the map. So, the next lookup is directly from the map and hence faster. The `IdentityMap` pattern has been implemented in Mongoid (and removed in the latest version).

 Ignore the rest of this section if you use Mongoid4. Only if you are using Mongoid 3, is the remaining section relevant.

If enabled properly, `IdentityMap` can greatly improve the performance of queries. Whenever a document is loaded from the database, it is classified by class and ID kept in the `IdentityMap` pattern. Then, when that document is looked up the next time, Mongoid looks into the `IdentityMap` pattern before looking into the database.

So, how do we know that the `IdentityMap` pattern is there? First, enable it.

```
# config/mongoid.yml

development:
  sessions:
    ...
  options:
    identity_map_enabled: true
```

Now, let's see how this works on the console:

```
irb> Mongoid::IdentityMap
 => {}


irb> Book.first
 => #<Book _id: 516e7ab045db7cd86a000001, t(title): "Aristortle",
published_date: 2012-05-20 00:00:00 UTC, author_id: nil, category_ids:
nil>


irb> Mongoid::IdentityMap
 => {:books=>{"516e7ab045db7cd86a000001"=>#<Book _id:
516e7ab045db7cd86a000001, t(title): "Aristortle", published_date: 2012-
05-20 00:00:00 UTC, author_id: nil, category_ids: nil>}}


irb> Author.find("51b42d4245db7c9535000001")
```

```
=> #<Author _id: 51b42d4245db7c9535000001, name: "a4", last_name: nil,
wallet: nil, password: nil>
```

irb> Mongoid::IdentityMap

```
=> {:books=>{"516e7ab045db7cd86a000001"=>#<Book _id:
516e7ab045db7cd86a000001, t(title): "Aristortle", published_date: 2012-
05-20 00:00:00 UTC, author_id: nil, category_ids: nil>}, :authors=>{"51
b42d4245db7c9535000001"=>#<Author _id: 51b42d4245db7c9535000001, name:
"a4", last_name: nil, wallet: nil, password: nil>}}
```

Now, Mongoid will look into the IdentityMap pattern before looking up the database!

n+1 query problem and eager loading

So, what happens if we want to find the authors and list their books? Maybe, we could write some simple code like the following:

irb> Author.all.each { |a| p a, a.books.collect(&:title) }

```
=>  => [["Gautam", []], ["Gautam Rege", []], ["Gautam Rege2", []],
["Gautam Rege4", []], ["Nested Author", ["NB1", "NB2"]], ["Nested
Author1", []], ["Nested Author1", []], ["Nested Author1", []] ... ]
```

However, let's see how many queries were fired:

```
    MOPED: 127.0.0.1:27017 QUERY         database=sodibee_development
collection=authors selector={} flags=[:slave_ok] limit=0 skip=0 batch_
size=nil fields=nil (0.5822ms)
    MOPED: 127.0.0.1:27017 QUERY         database=sodibee_development
collection=books selector={"author_id"=>"515085fd45db7c911e000003"}
flags=[:slave_ok] limit=0 skip=0 batch_size=nil fields=nil (0.6301ms)
    MOPED: 127.0.0.1:27017 QUERY         database=sodibee_development
collection=books selector={"author_id"=>"518dfdcf45db7c6909000001"}
flags=[:slave_ok] limit=0 skip=0 batch_size=nil fields=nil (0.4430ms)
    MOPED: 127.0.0.1:27017 QUERY         database=sodibee_development
collection=books selector={"author_id"=>"518e562b0382dd6b5aba3afb"}
flags=[:slave_ok] limit=0 skip=0 batch_size=nil fields=nil (0.3400ms)
    MOPED: 127.0.0.1:27017 QUERY         database=sodibee_development
collection=books selector={"author_id"=>"518e56470382dd6b5aba3afc"}
flags=[:slave_ok] limit=0 skip=0 batch_size=nil fields=nil (0.3440ms)
```

Basically, one query is fired to fetch all the authors and then another query for fetching the books of each author. So, if there are 10 authors, 11 queries are fired. Though this seems fine at first, imagine what happens if there are 50,000 authors or maybe five million authors.

This is called the **n+1** query problem. To resolve this, we fire one query to find the authors and an `$in` query to find all the books of those authors. This is called **eager loading**. Let's see how that's done:

```
irb> Author.all.includes(:books).collect { |a| p a.name, a.books.
collect(&:title) }
 => ["Gautam Rege4", []], ["Nested Author", ["NB1", "NB2"]], ["Nested
Author1", []], ["Nested Author1", []], ["Nested Author1", []] ... ]
```

Same result! However, let's look at how many queries got fired: only and always 2, irrespective of whether there are 10 authors or 5 million.

```
   MOPED: 127.0.0.1:27017 QUERY          database=sodibee_development
collection=authors selector={} flags=[:slave_ok] limit=0 skip=0 batch_
size=nil fields=nil (0.7982ms)

   MOPED: 127.0.0.1:27017 QUERY          database=sodibee_development
collection=books selector={"author_id"=>{"$in"=>["515085fd45db7c91
1e000003", "518dfdcf45db7c6909000001", "518e562b0382dd6b5aba3afb",
"518e56470382dd6b5aba3afc", "519ae2b945db7c29cd00000e",
"519ae45b45db7c540a000011", "519ae4e745db7cddd0000012",
"519ae4f845db7cddd0000014", "519ae6db45db7cdd7c000018",
"519b0dce45db7c44e4000025", "519ba17d45db7c5ac9000005",
"51b4296a45db7cf6c0000002", "51b42a5645db7c6c83000001",
"51b42ae345db7c6c83000002", "51b42d4245db7c9535000001",
"5143678345db7ca255000001"]}} flags=[:slave_ok] limit=0 skip=0 batch_
size=nil fields=nil (35.4841ms)
```

 Eager loading is now an integral part of Mongoid and the entire `IdentityMap` has been removed from the source.

MapReduce and the aggregation framework

MapReduce is a concept: we *map* data into multiple independent tasks, process the temporary results, and *reduce* the results in parallel. Basically, we spawn many parallel tasks to mappers. These mappers (which can be threads, processes, or servers, among others) process a specific dataset and spew out results to the reducers. As the reducers keep getting information, they update the final results with this data. This is basically the *divide and conquer* process.

Nothing explains this better than an example! Suppose we want to show the statistical count of authors by the first letter of their name; it is a good case for using MapReduce. We want to see information as follows:

```
Authors starting with "a": 1020
Authors starting with "b": 477
Authors starting with "c": 719
Authors starting with "d": 586
Authors starting with "e": 678
```

First, let's create many authors in our database. For this, we shall use the `faker` gem so that we can generate nice names. We can use the `rake` task to generate 10,000 authors. This is written in a `rake` type, for example, `lib/tasks/fake_authors.rake`.

```
require 'faker'

task :fake_authors => :environment do
  10000.times do
    a = Author.create(:name => "#{Faker::Name.first_name}
#{Faker::Name.last_name}")
  end
end
```

To run this, we simply issue the command as follows:

```
$ bundle exec rake fake_authors
```

```
irb > Author.limit(5).collect(&:name)
 => ["Victor Metz", "Dayana Rau", "Ada Wiza", "Price Osinski", "Virgie
Hand"]
```

```
> Author.count
 => 10016
```

Now, let's write the `map` and `reduce` functions in Ruby. It's important to remember that MongoDB allows us to use only JavaScript for custom functions, so we need these functions to be JavaScript. Since we cannot directly write JavaScript in our Ruby code, we wrap the JavaScript functions as strings and send them as parameters to MongoDB.

```
map = %q{function() {
        emit(this.name.toLowerCase()[0], {count:1});
      }
}

reduce = %q{function(key, values) {
```

```
                    var r = { count: 0 };
                    values.forEach(function(value) {
                        r.count += value.count;
                    })
                    return r;
                }
            }
```

A closer look reveals that the map function emits the first character of the author's name and a count, which is 1.

The `reduce` function receives a key and an array of values, each containing a result. This is how MapReduce works:

- The `map` function emits a key and a count. So, if we take the case of four authors, "Samuel", "Sameer", "Gautam", and "Shawn", there will be four emits, one for each document: `('s', 1), ('s', 1), ('g', 1),` and `('s', 1)`.

- Due to the evented nature of JavaScript, as each `map` function emits the value, it is handled by a reducer, but in no particular order.

- There are always as many `map` functions invoked as the number of documents that are processed. However, there could be a lesser number of `reduce` function calls.

- Suppose the first two emits were received, the `reduce` function will get the parameters `('s', [1, 1])` and as we can see, it aggregates the value and returns 2. The `reducer` function now emits (just like a `map` function): `('s', 2)`.

- Now, another `reduce` function receives `('g', [1])` and emits `('g', 1)`.

- When the next `('s', 1)` is emitted, it is received by another `reduce` function as `('s', [1])` and it emits `('s', 1)`.

- Now, another `reduce` method gets called with `('s', [2, 1])`, that is, the result of the previous `reduce` functions, and a result is emitted: `('s', 3)`.

- Finally, when there is nothing to be reduced, the result is aggregated as `{'s': 3, 'g': 1}`.

Now, let's see how we trigger the MapReduce on our authors:

```
irb> res = Author.map_reduce(map, reduce).out(replace: "stats")
 => => #<Mongoid::Contextual::MapReduce
  selector: {}
  class:    Author
  map:      function() {
                emit(this.name.toLowerCase()[0], {count:1});
```

```
        }

    reduce:    function(key, values) {
                  var r = { count: 0 };

                  values.forEach(function(value) {
                     r.count += value.count;
                  })
                  return r;
               }


    finalize:
    out:        {:replace=>"res"}
```

Now, let's see what the results have in store for us:

```
irb> res.each { |d| p d }
{"_id"=>"a", "value"=>{"count"=>976.0}}
{"_id"=>"b", "value"=>{"count"=>496.0}}
{"_id"=>"c", "value"=>{"count"=>710.0}}
{"_id"=>"d", "value"=>{"count"=>692.0}}
{"_id"=>"e", "value"=>{"count"=>645.0}}
{"_id"=>"f", "value"=>{"count"=>238.0}}
{"_id"=>"g", "value"=>{"count"=>387.0}}
{"_id"=>"h", "value"=>{"count"=>306.0}}
{"_id"=>"i", "value"=>{"count"=>147.0}}
{"_id"=>"j", "value"=>{"count"=>792.0}}
{"_id"=>"k", "value"=>{"count"=>555.0}}
{"_id"=>"l", "value"=>{"count"=>596.0}}
{"_id"=>"m", "value"=>{"count"=>907.0}}
{"_id"=>"n", "value"=>{"count"=>265.0}}
{"_id"=>"o", "value"=>{"count"=>200.0}}
{"_id"=>"p", "value"=>{"count"=>180.0}}
{"_id"=>"q", "value"=>{"count"=>24.0}}
{"_id"=>"r", "value"=>{"count"=>532.0}}
{"_id"=>"s", "value"=>{"count"=>510.0}}
{"_id"=>"t", "value"=>{"count"=>349.0}}
```

```
{"_id"=>"u", "value"=>{"count"=>20.0}}
{"_id"=>"v", "value"=>{"count"=>204.0}}
{"_id"=>"w", "value"=>{"count"=>157.0}}
{"_id"=>"x", "value"=>{"count"=>10.0}}
{"_id"=>"y", "value"=>{"count"=>46.0}}
{"_id"=>"z", "value"=>{"count"=>72.0}}
 => #<Enumerator: #<Moped::Cursor:0x007fb07d29c2e8 @
session=<Moped::Session seeds=["localhost:27017"] database=sodibee_
development>, @database="sodibee_development", @collection="res", @
selector={}, @cursor_id=0, @limit=0, @limited=false, @batch_size=0, @
options={:request_id=>0, :flags=>[:slave_ok], :limit=>0, :skip=>0,
:fields=>nil}, @node=<Moped::Node resolved_address="127.0.0.1:27017">>:ea
ch>
```

Understandably, the results were pretty quick; much faster than iterating 10,000 authors. And just how much time did this take?

```
irb> res.counts
 => {"input"=>10016, "emit"=>10016, "reduce"=>792, "output"=>26}
```

As we can also see, the number of `emit` is the same as the number of documents processed; but the number of times the `reduce` function was invoked is only `792`.

Important things to remember when using MapReduce

The `map` function works only on a single document at a time. In the `map` function, we cannot query the database or access any other documents. Think of this *only* as a JavaScript function that has been passed a JSON document.

The `map` function should be **idempotent**. This means that even if the function is called multiple times with the same value, it should return the same result.

Using the aggregation framework

The aggregation framework does not replace MapReduce. The aggregation framework is useful when we are trying to get consolidated results, for example, the count of authors. Aggregations can also be used to simulate the GROUP BY query fragment.

Mongoid now uses the aggregation framework instead of MapReduce to get the counts. It currently supports only the basic aggregations: :count, :min, :max, :sum, and :avg.

Let's see an example. Suppose we wanted to get all the aggregations of authors using MapReduce, this is what we would do (this reference is from an older Mongoid library):

```
mapper = %Q{
            function() {
              var agg = {
              count: 1,
              max: this.#{field},
              min: this.#{field},
              sum: this.#{field}
              };
              emit("#{field}", agg);
          }}
```

Here, the `field` variable is `:id` by default. However, we can get results on any field in the document. The `reducer` function is given as follows:

```
reducer = %Q{

      function(key, values) {
        var agg = { count: 0, max: null, min: null, sum: 0 };
        values.forEach(function(val) {
          if (val.max !== null) {
            if (agg.max == null || val.max > agg.max) agg.max = val.
max;
            if (agg.min == null || val.max < agg.min) agg.min = val.
max;

            agg.sum += val.sum;
          }
          agg.count += val.count;
        });
        return agg;
      }}
```

Let's see how we use them:

```
irb> r = Author.map_reduce(mapper(:id), reducer).out(inline: 1)

irb> r.execute

=> {"results"=>[{"_id"=>"id", "value"=>{"count"=>10016.0, "max"=>nil,
"min"=>nil, "sum"=>0.0}}], "timeMillis"=>415, "counts"=>{"input"=>10016,
"emit"=>10016, "reduce"=>101, "output"=>1}, "ok"=>1.0}
```

Now if you see, this has taken 415 ms. If we look at the logs, this is the command that got fired:

```
MOPED: 127.0.0.1:27017 COMMAND        database=sodibee_development
command={:mapreduce=>"authors", :map=>"\n            function() {\n
var agg = {\n            count: 1,\n            max: this.
id,\n          min: this.id,\n            sum: this.id\n
};\n          emit(\"id\", agg);\n          }", :reduce=>"\n
function(key, values) {\n          var agg = { count: 0, max: null,
min: null, sum: 0 };\n          values.forEach(function(val) {\n
if (val.max !== null) {\n          if (agg.max == null || val.
max > agg.max) agg.max = val.max;\n            if (agg.min ==
null || val.max < agg.min) agg.min = val.max;\n          agg.
sum += val.sum;\n          }\n          agg.count += val.
count;\n            });\n          return agg;\n          }",
:query=>{}, :out=>{:inline=>1}} (414.4499ms)
```

Now, let's see how the aggregation framework works instead:

```
irb> Author.collection.aggregate.count
 => 10016
```

Let's see what was in the logs:

```
MOPED: 127.0.0.1:27017 COMMAND        database=sodibee_development
command={:aggregate=>"authors", :pipeline=>[]} (94.5258ms)
```

This has taken only 94 ms.

Now let's see how our Mongoid calls, which is similar to ActiveModel:

```
> Author.count
 => 10016
```

And the following query got fired:

```
MOPED: 127.0.0.1:27017 COMMAND        database=sodibee_development
command={:count=>"authors", :query=>{}} (0.6540ms)
```

The query took 0.6 ms. What's happening here is as follows:

- MapReduce is eventually JavaScript. Although it works in an evented manner, it still processes each document and emits some result. Hence, it takes more time and completes in 415 ms.

- Aggregation is deep inside the MongoDB core, that is, C++ compiled code. So, it's very fast and has access to internal document storage.

- Lastly, Mongoid caches results if there are no changes to the documents. That is why when we call `Author.count`, the result is returned from cache.

Choosing between MapReduce and the aggregation framework

This is a question that often crops up when we have to get quicker and faster results. There is no perfect answer but I recommend the following:

If you require consolidated numbers or grouping with no data manipulation, try to use the aggregation framework to get your results; if that is not feasible, use MapReduce.

In the previous example, we saw that we were trying to get the consolidated numbers of authors; but we were manipulating information — we wanted the count of authors by the first letter of their names. So, MapReduce was the right choice.

When we are trying to get a `count`, `min`, `max`, or `average` of some field in the `Author` model, we should use the aggregation framework. The aggregation framework has a pipeline that supports the operators shown in the following table:

Operator	Meaning and example
`$project`	This is the document stream. This is similar to `SELECT` in SQL, but it can manipulate the data stream.
`$match`	This filters the document. This is similar to `WHERE` in SQL and to the MongoDB query syntax.
`$limit`	This limits the number of documents being passed in the pipeline.
`$skip`	This skips some documents in the pipeline and returns the rest.
`$sort`	This sorts the documents in the pipeline.
`$unwind`	This coverts elements of an array into documents and returns them as a document stream.
`$group`	This is similar to `GROUP BY` and collects documents for calculating the aggregates of the collection.
`$geoNear`	This returns results based on geospatial indexing.

Monitoring query performance

MongoDB provides a lot of tools for monitoring performance of the database. By default, it is configured to log only slow queries — those that consume more than 100 ms in database operations. It's very important to monitor these logs.

If you see any `query` commands taking a long time, in most cases it means that the fields need to be indexed as follows:

```
[conn23] query sodibee_development.authors query: { $query: { ... }
ntoreturn:10 ntoskip:0 nscanned:17158 scanAndOrder:1 keyUpdates:0
numYields: 1 locks(micros)  r:272157 nreturned:10 reslen:20221 169m
```

This query log has some interesting information as shown in the following table:

Expression	Description
[conn32]	This is the client connection.
query	This is the command that was fired. It can be insert, update, and so on.
sodibee_ development. authors	This is the database and the collection on which this query was fired.
{ $query: { ... }	This is the actual query that was fired.
ntoreturn	This is 1000 unless limit is used in the query.
ntoskip	This is 0 unless skip is used in the query.
nsanned	This is the entire document set that was scanned.
scanAndOrder, keyUpdate	These are used internally. keyUpdate tells us the number of indexes that were updated. scanAndOrder is to identify whether documents can be sorted according to their order in the index.
nreturned	This is the number of objects returned.
numYields	This is the number of times the query yielded the read lock and the amount of time the lock was held (microseconds).
reslen	This is the number of bytes of the result and the time taken in ms.

Among these logs, the most important is the time taken. Typically, if the database query is over 100 ms, there is a need to optimize the query — usually by adding indexes. As we have seen earlier, explain is an excellent method to check what the query performance will be.

 The other tools that help in monitoring MongoDB are part of **MongoDB Management Services** (**MMS**), which is provided as a premium service by MongoDB. If you also want to monitor the Rails app, I recommend using **New Relic RPM**.

Profiling MongoDB

We can monitor the performance of MongoDB by enabling profiling.

There are three modes of profiling:

- 0: This indicates profiling is disabled
- -1: (no change) This returns the current profile level
- 1: This indicates profiling is suited to write only slow operations
- 2: This indicates profiling is suited to write all operations

Even if profiling is disabled, the slow queries (the ones taking longer than 100 ms by default) get logged in the MongoDB log file.

We can configure profiling either from the console or as a startup command to MongoDB, as follows:

```
mongo> db.setProfilingLevel(1)
    { "was" : 0, "slowms" : 100, "ok" : 1 }
mongo>
```

Alternatively, we can enable profiling on the command line using `--profile=1`. The `slowms` option tells MongoDB what should be the threshold time for slow queries. The `was` field tells us what the earlier profiling level was. Now, let's see a `profile` log. Execute the following command:

```
mongo> db.system.profile.find()
{ "ts" : ISODate("2012-06-08T07:26:43.186Z"),
  "op" : "query", "ns" : "sodibee_development.authors",
  "query" : { "name" : /ou/ }, "nscanned" : 609, "nreturned" : 101,
  "responseLength" : 6613, "millis" : 10, "client" : "127.0.0.1",
  "user": ""
}
```

In the preceding command, the `op` and `ns` parameters specify the operation and the collection that was profiled. The `query` parameter logs the query that was fired. The `nscanned` parameter specifies the number of objects that were scanned for fetching the result. The `nreturned` parameter specifies the number of objects in the result.

The `responseLength` or `reslen` parameter specifies the number of bytes in the result and the `millis` parameter indicates the time in milliseconds taken by MongoDB for processing this query.

Statistical data

So, how do we find out the statistical data about our database?

```
mongo> db.stats()
  "db" : "sodibee_development",
  "collections" : 9,
  "objects" : 10164,
  "avgObjSize" : 51.66036993309721,
  "dataSize" : 525076,
```

```
  "storageSize" : 2494464,
  "numExtents" : 13,
  "indexes" : 12,
  "indexSize" : 1103760,
  "fileSize" : 201326592,
  "nsSizeMB" : 16,
  "dataFileVersion" : {
    "major" : 4,
    "minor" : 6
  },
  "ok" : 1
}
```

And if we want to find out statistical data about a particular collection, we can do that too:

```
mongo> db.authors.stats() {
  "ns" : "sodibee_development.authors",
  "count" : 10016,
  "size" : 489984,
  "avgObjSize" : 48.92012779552716,
  "storageSize" : 1396736,
  "numExtents" : 5,
  "nindexes" : 4,
  "lastExtentSize" : 1048576,
  "paddingFactor" : 1.0000000000000013,
  "systemFlags" : 1,
  "userFlags" : 0,
  "totalIndexSize" : 1038352,
  "indexSizes" : {
    "_id_" : 335216,
    "address.location_2d" : 8176,
    "address.location_2dsphere_address.city_1" : 367920,
    "name_1" : 327040
  },
  "ok" : 1
}
```

Hint and currentOp

MongoDB tries to infer the ideal index to use for the queries. However, we can choose to override this and provide MongoDB a hint about which index to use. We can specify the index directly or by its name.

Sometimes, we may fire a long-running query that could slow down our database access. Alternatively, we may want to see what operation is currently being executed by the database. Mongoid does not support direct access to currentOp. So, to check on this, we have to access the database via the MongoDB client.

Good practices and recommendations

Here are some of the best practices that should be followed while working with MongoDB:

- Use indexing judiciously. Try to keep multikey indexes such that we do not need to duplicate indexes. Database writes are slowed down with lots of indexes, but reads could be fast. We need to strike the right balance.

- Use the aggregation framework as often as possible. Remember Mongoid caches results for even better performance.

- MapReduce is a great tool to get faster aggregated results. However, you cannot use it with multiple collections.

- Know when to use Text indexes, it's fine for really simple searches but not good if you want complex facet queries. If you require complex facet queries, I recommend looking at ElasticSearch.

- Use the hash index for basic field searches, but not for multikey searches as we have seen.

- Keep an eye out for slow queries.

Summary

Mongoid relies a lot on MongoDB for performance. We leverage the features of MongoDB, such as MapReduce and the aggregation framework, that give us a huge performance boost. Indexing is the easiest and ideal means of ensuring that our queries are fast.

Performance tuning is a continuous process, and we should keep monitoring our servers and databases to find and optimize slow queries.

In the next chapter, we shall see the different modules and gems that are supported, which give our application additional functionality as well as make our life easier.

7
Mongoid Modules

Now that we have seen how to use Mongoid and its various features, let's look at some modules and gems that enhance the capabilities of our applications using Mongoid. Some of these modules can simply be turned on, and some are gems that need to be installed.

We shall see how modules such as Paranoia, Timestamping, and Versioning can help us manage data. We shall also discuss some gems that can be used with Mongoid for managing a state machine, authentication, uploading files, and even creating an audit trail.

Let's take the plunge!

Timestamping

This is pretty straightforward. When you require the created-at and updated-at timestamps, simply include this module in the model as follows:

```
class Book
  include Mongoid::Document
  include Mongoid::Timestamps
end
```

This adds the `created_at` and `updated_at` datetime fields to the document.

Versioning

Often, the need arises to maintain different versions of a document. The **Versioning** module has been removed from Mongoid 4.0 and put into a separate gem. So, to enable Versioning, we need to include the `mongoid-versioning` gem in our `Gemfile`.

We can turn on Versioning by simply including it in our class, as shown in the following code snippet:

```
class Contact
    include Mongoid::Document
    include Mongoid::Versioning
    ...
end
```

Using Versioning is simple enough, we don't really have to do anything, as shown in the following code snippet:

```
irb> b = Book.new(title: "Legend of Ross")

 => #<Book _id: 528a920b47617552c7010000, version: 1, t(title): "Legend
of Ross", price: nil, page_count: nil, published_date: nil, is_best_
seller: false, awards: [], isbn: nil, status: nil, reserved: nil,
reserved_on: nil, reserved_by: nil, reserved_count: nil, currency: nil,
author_id: nil>


irb> b.save

 => true


irb> b.versions

 => []


irb> b.price = 99.99

 => 99.99


irb> b.save

 => true


irb> b.versions

 => [#<Book _id: , version: 1, t(title): "Legend of Ross", price: nil,
page_count: nil, published_date: nil, is_best_seller: false, awards: [],
isbn: nil, status: nil, reserved: nil, reserved_on: nil, reserved_by:
nil, reserved_count: nil, currency: nil, author_id: nil>]
```

Remember that `versions` is a type of embedded relation (namely `embeds_many`). So if the document gets saved very often, it could lead to the document becoming really huge! To avoid that, we can cap the maximum number of versions that should be stored.

```
Book.max_versions(10)
```

Sometimes, we want to control the Versioning. If we do not want to save a version when the object is modified, we can do so very simply as shown in the following code snippet:

```
b.versionless do
  b.page_count = 100
  b.save
end
```

This will save the object but not version it. On the other extreme, if we want to save the object as a new version even if it hasn't changed, we can do that too, as shown in the following code snippet:

```
> b.revise!
 => true
```

Remember that Mongoid does not save the document if there are no changes to it. In spite of that, we can revise the document as follows:

```
> b.version
 => 2
```

```
> b.save
 => true
```

```
> c.version
 => 4
```

```
> b.revise!
 => true
```

```
> b.changes
 => {}
```

```
> b.version
 => 5
```

Paranoia

As the name suggests, there are times when we never want data to be really deleted from the database, but simply marked for deletion. This is indeed paranoid, but is required for data-sensitive applications where we need to keep a track of all documents, even when they are deleted. The **Paranoia** module has been removed from Mongoid 4.0 and put into a separate gem. So, to enable it, we need to include the `mongoid-paranoia` gem in our `Gemfile`.

Here is a simple example:

```
class Book
  include Mongoid::Document
  include Mongoid::Paranoia
end
```

Let's see how this works, as shown in the following code snippet:

```
irb> b = Book.last

=> #<Book _id: 51d579e245db7c6a66000001, deleted_at: nil, t(title):
"test" author_id: "51b42d4245db7c9535000001 >


irb> b.delete
 => true


irb> Book.where(id: '51d579e245db7c6a66000001').first
 => nil


irb> Book.unscoped.where(id: '51d579e245db7c6a66000001').first

 => #<Book _id: 51d579e245db7c6a66000001, deleted_at: 2013-08-24 15:25:48
UTC, t(title): "test", author_id: "51b42d4245db7c9535000001>
```

As we can see, when we deleted the book document, it did not really get deleted but had a new `deleted_at` timestamp added instead. When we include the Paranoia module, a new default scope `deleted_at: nil` is added. So whenever we fetch documents, the ones that have the `deleted_at` timestamp are not fetched. If we really want to query all the documents, we simply use the `unscoped` scope.

Acts as state machine (aasm)

A **finite-state machine** (**FSM**) is based on the concept of an object being in a particular state and then transitioning to other states based on certain events. Let's take the example of reserving a book. The states that the reservation can be in are `available`, `booked`, and `late`. For this example, the reservation can transition to these states in any of the following ways:

- All books have a single reservation each
- The default status of a reservation is `available`
- A customer can reserve a book if it's `available`
- A customer can return a book if it's `booked` or it's `late`
- A book is delayed if it's reserved for more than the default seven days

To use the state machine, we need to add the `aasm` gem into `Gemfile` as follows:

```
class Reservation
  include Mongoid::Document
  include AASM

  field :aasm_state, type: String
  field :booked_on, type: Date
  field booked_by, type: String
  field :returned_on, type: Date
  field :days_reserved, type: Integer, default: 7

  belongs_to :book

  aasm do
    state :available, initial: true
    state :booked
    state :late

    event :reserve_book do
      before { self.booked_on = Date.today }

      transitions from: :available, to: :booked
    end

    event :return_book do
      after { self.returned_on = Date.today }

      transitions from: :booked, to: :available
```

```
          transitions from: :late, to: :available
      end

      event :book_delay do
          transitions from: :booked, to: :late, guard: :is_late?
      end
    end

    def is_late?
      Date.today > booked_on + days_reserved
    end
  end
```

Now, let's play with this as follows:

```
irb> b = Book.create(title: "Mount of County Mistro")

=> #<Book _id: 528acbb347617502cc000000, version: 1, deleted_at:
nil, t(title): "Mount of County Mistro", price: nil, page_count: nil,
published_date: nil, is_best_seller: false, awards: [], isbn: nil,
status: nil, reserved: nil, reserved_on: nil, reserved_by: nil, reserved_
count: nil, currency: nil, author_id: nil>
```

```
irb> b.create_reservation(booked_by: "Gautam")

=> #<Reservation _id: 528acbbc47617502cc010000, aasm_state: "available",
booked_on: nil, booked_by: "Gautam", returned_on: nil, days_reserved: 7,
book_id: BSON::ObjectId('528acbb347617502cc000000')>
```

We can see that the default state of the reservation is `available`. Lets reserve it.

```
> b.reservation.reserve_book!

=> true
```

```
> b.reservation

=> #<Reservation _id: 528acbbc47617502cc010000, aasm_state: "booked",
booked_on: 2013-11-18 00:00:00 UTC, booked_by: "Gautam", returned_
on: nil, days_reserved: 7, book_id: BSON::ObjectId('528acbb347617502
cc000000')
```

We can see that the `aasm_state` is now `booked` and the `booked_on` field is updated. Now, let's see how an invalid transition is prevented using `aasm`:

```
> b.reservation.book_delay!

AASM::InvalidTransition: Event 'book_delay' cannot transition from
'booked'
```

This happens because of the guard that we have kept to ensure that a book is `late` only if the `booked_on` date is older than seven days.

Play around with `AASM` and use it when you want to manage different states. If it were not for `AASM`, we would have to manage the state transitions using the `if...else` conditions, and then if we needed to change any transitions, it would be a nightmare! You will find the latest information on the `aasm` gem at `https://github.com/aasm/aasm`.

carrierwave

Often, we need to upload files such as profile photos, documents, and so on. The ideal gem to manage this is `carrierwave`. It works easily with Mongoid and can store data on the local filesystem, as well as in a cloud such as AWS S3.

You will find more details about `carrierwave` at `https://github.com/carrierwaveuploader/carrierwave-mongoid`.

mongoid-audit

Sometimes we need to audit our documents. This means that we need to log details of the changes to documents when they were created or updated. We need to log timestamps, user details, what was modified, and what were the original values.

The `mongoid-audit` gem makes this very trivial. It maintains a collection named `history_trackers` that keeps a track of the entire history of a document. Using it, we can easily configure the fields and actions we want to audit.

More details are available at `https://github.com/rs-pro/mongoid-audit`.

devise

The `devise` gem is used for authentication. It seamlessly integrates with Mongoid and provides the functionality of registration and login. Some wonderfully configurable modules that it has are as follows:

- **Trackable**: This keeps a track of login details such as login count, IP address, and last logged
- **Confirmable**: This sends a confirmation e-mail during registration
- **Rememberable**: This keeps the user logged in across multiple sessions just like the **Remember me** checkbox we see on a lot of websites
- **Recoverable**: This helps recover passwords

- **Lockable**: This locks the account after a certain number of failed attempts
- **OpenAuthentication and Single Sign On support**: This is provided with token authentication

More details are available at `https://github.com/plataformatec/devise`.

Summary

In this chapter, we saw how we can enhance Mongoid using certain modules and gems. These gems help us build applications faster and make them stable.

I do hope you have enjoyed reading the book as much as I have enjoyed writing it!

Index

Symbols

$geoNear 82, 105
$group 105
$limit 105
$match 81, 105
$project 81, 105
{ $query: { ... } expression 106
$skip 105
$sort 81, 105
$sum 81
$unwind 81, 105
:after_add option 54
:after_remove option 54
:all 70
:allow_destroy object 43
:as option 49, 50
:autobuild option 49, 51
:autosave option 49, 51
:before_add option 54
:before_remove option 54
:cascaded_callbacks option 49, 65
:class_name option 48
[conn32] expression 106
:counter_cache option 49, 56, 57
:cyclic option 49, 66
:delete value 51
:dependent option
  :delete value 51
  :destroy value 51
  :nullify value 51
  :restrict value 51
  about 49, 51
:destroy value 51
:each 73
:elem_match 71

:exists 71
:exists? 73
:extend option 48
:find 73
:find_and_modify 78
:find_by 73
:find_or_create_by 73
:find_or_initialize_by 73
:first 73
:first_or_create 73
:first_or_create! 73
:first_or_initialize 73
:following relation 62
:foreign_key option 49, 52
%gt/%gte/%lt/%lte, query selectors 71
:in 71
:index option 49, 55
:inverse_class_name option 48
:inverse_of option 48, 58-62
:last 73
:limit object 43
:name option 48
:near 71
:near_sphere 71
:nin 71
:nullify value 51
:order option 49
:polymorphic option 49, 56
:primary_key option 49, 51, 52
:reject_if object 42
:relation option 48
:restrict value 51
:store_as option 49, 65
:touch option 49, 56
:validate option 49, 52
:versioned option 49

:foreign_key option 49
:index option 49
:order option 49
:polymorphic option 49
:primary_key option 49
:store_as option 49
:touch option 49
:validate option 49
:versioned option 49
reslen expression 106
resource_id field 51
resource_type field 51
Ruby version 8

S

save! function 38
serialization 21, 22
serialize method 21
Sodibee
  about 7
  functions 7
  prerequisites 8
  setting up 9, 10
sodibee_development.authors
      expression 106
Sodibee, prerequisites
  MongoDB version 9

Ruby version 8
Sodibee, setting up
  models, creating 11
  models, testing 12
strong_parameters 31
Symbol class
  overloading 72

T

text index 93, 95
time attributes 20
timestamping 111

U

upsert action 38

V

validates_associated method 52
validation
  URL 43
Vehicle model
  designing 63
versioning 111-113

Thank you for buying
Learning Mongoid

About Packt Publishing

Packt, pronounced 'packed', published its first book "*Mastering phpMyAdmin for Effective MySQL Management*" in April 2004 and subsequently continued to specialize in publishing highly focused books on specific technologies and solutions.

Our books and publications share the experiences of your fellow IT professionals in adapting and customizing today's systems, applications, and frameworks. Our solution based books give you the knowledge and power to customize the software and technologies you're using to get the job done. Packt books are more specific and less general than the IT books you have seen in the past. Our unique business model allows us to bring you more focused information, giving you more of what you need to know, and less of what you don't.

Packt is a modern, yet unique publishing company, which focuses on producing quality, cutting-edge books for communities of developers, administrators, and newbies alike. For more information, please visit our website: www.packtpub.com.

About Packt Open Source

In 2010, Packt launched two new brands, Packt Open Source and Packt Enterprise, in order to continue its focus on specialization. This book is part of the Packt Open Source brand, home to books published on software built around Open Source licenses, and offering information to anybody from advanced developers to budding web designers. The Open Source brand also runs Packt's Open Source Royalty Scheme, by which Packt gives a royalty to each Open Source project about whose software a book is sold.

Writing for Packt

We welcome all inquiries from people who are interested in authoring. Book proposals should be sent to author@packtpub.com. If your book idea is still at an early stage and you would like to discuss it first before writing a formal book proposal, contact us; one of our commissioning editors will get in touch with you.

We're not just looking for published authors; if you have strong technical skills but no writing experience, our experienced editors can help you develop a writing career, or simply get some additional reward for your expertise.

Instant MongoDB

ISBN: 978-1-78216-970-3   Paperback: 72 pages

Get up to speed with one of the world's most popular NoSQL database

1. Learn something new in an Instant! A short, fast, focused guide delivering immediate results

2. Query in MongoDB from the Mongo shell

3. Learn about the aggregation framework and Map Reduce support in Mongo

4. Tips and tricks for schema designing and how to develop high performance applications using MongoDB

Ruby and MongoDB Web Development Beginner's Guide

ISBN: 978-1-84951-502-3   Paperback: 332 pages

Create dynamic web applications by combining the power of Ruby and MongoDB

1. Step-by-step instructions and practical examples to creating web applications with Ruby and MongoDB

2. Learn to design the object model in a NoSQL way

3. Create objects in Ruby and map them to MongoDB

Please check **www.PacktPub.com** for information on our titles

PHP and MongoDB Web Development Beginner's Guide

ISBN: 978-1-84951-362-3   Paperback: 292 pages

Combine the power of PHP and MongoDB to build dynamic web 2.0 applications

1. Learn to build PHP-powered dynamic web applications using MongoDB as the data backend

2. Handle user sessions, store real-time site analytics, build location-aware web apps, and much more, all using MongoDB and PHP

3. Full of step-by-step instructions and practical examples, along with challenges to test and improve your knowledge

CouchDB and PHP Web Development Beginner's Guide

ISBN: 978-1-84951-358-6   Paperback: 304 pages

Get your PHP applications from conception to deployment by leveraging CouchDB's robust features

1. Build and deploy a flexible Social Networking application using PHP and leveraging key features of CouchDB to do the heavy lifting

2. Explore the features and functionality of CouchDB, by taking a deep look into Documents, Views, Replication, and much more.

3. Conceptualize a lightweight PHP framework from scratch and write code that can easily port to other frameworks

Please check **www.PacktPub.com** for information on our titles